Just Because

Gregory M. Dixon

978-1-965552-36-0 (Paperback)
978-1-965552-37-7 (Hardback)
978-1-965552-38-4 (E-book)

Library of Congress Control Number: 2025916582

BOOKWRIGHTS
HOUSE

admin@bookwrightshouse.com
☎ (213) 286 6700

Table of Contents

Jesus once said,
"In my Father's house are many mansions."
As a servant of the Lord, will my work speak for me?

Acknowledgments

My wife, Wanda, and I have been married for twenty-seven years. We have three beautiful kids; they are Gabriel, thirty-five; Sharonda, thirty-five; and Michael, thirty. We are also proud grandparents.

In addition to my family, I must extend a special honor to Mrs. Crycynthia Gardner and Cynthia Border. They gave positive feedback and encouraged me early in my songwriting. I must not forget about their spouses, Pastor John Gardner Sr. and Deacon John Border, for supporting their wives; it was a previous pastor, Dr. General Bryant, who planted the seed for me to write.

During Dr. Bryant's tenure at Second Elizabeth, I never missed a Sunday at tending church.

I would like to also thank Dr. Clarissa West-White. I am forever thankful for the godsent people in my life, and no amount of words could express the love that I have in my heart for them.

Special thanks to the churches in the following areas:

Steward Temple AME Church: 85 Woodward Rd., Quincy

Greenshade AME Church: 8152 Salem Rd., Quincy

St. Hebron AME Church: 1730 St. Hebron Rd., Quincy

St. John's AME Church: 4445 Bainbridge Rd., Quincy

Mt. Hosea Missionary Baptist Church: 1212 Mt. Hosea Church Rd, Quincy

Mt. Calvary Primitive Baptist Church: 7095 Bainbridge Rd., Quincy

Church of God in Christ: St. John, Quincy

St. Paul Primitive Baptist Church: 4562 Fowlstown Rd., Attapulgus

Mt. Zion Primitive Baptist Church: 20 S 9th Street, Quincy

Friendship Primitive Baptist Church: 5775 Ben Bostick Rd., Quincy

I have visited the above churches for Sunday services, funerals, revivals, and weddings. The atmosphere of each was very loving; revisitation was extended and well received. I would gladly call my church any one of the above churches.

Introduction

I was born in March of 1961 to the late Clarence Dixon and Lonnie Mae Murray-Dixon. My surviving siblings are Rodney Dixon, Joan Carol Dixon-Bridges (Evan), W. Dean Dixon-McClurkin (Melvin), and S. Latonya Dixon. Myself, brother, and three sisters are the sole survivors out of eight. Rose and Trenda were my sisters who passed early in my childhood. Those two sisters never learned to talk good and were plagued with health issues. They would cry and be standing in a bed of ants, while playing in the yard. I had to remove them from harm and remove the ants. I would rub them down with alcohol, as taught to do so. At eight years old, I realized that there was a God, and he is merciful.

One other sister passed at about two weeks old; she was my mother's firstborn. I am the fourth oldest out of my mother and father's children. In 1979, after graduating from high school, I enlisted in the United States Navy. After a total of twelve years of obligated service, my parents became sickly, and I later became a federal correctional officer in Tallahassee, Florida, for fourteen years.

Early in my youth, my parents were lacking in education, but not in love for me and my siblings. In my community, we were also loved; there was this household saying: "A community raises a child." I've found that to be true, due to the fact that my community had plenty of loving moms and dads. There were six moms who stood out; only five of them were coworkers with my mom. Their names are Mary Green, Matilda Sherman, Evelyn Zackery, Bessie

Mae Barkley, Mary Anderson, and Helen Carol. Only two of them are deceased now, but my memories of them will last forever. Families such as the Scotts, Kenons, Moyes, Lightfoots, Wiggins, Dinards, Haynes, and Thomases were the type of people that look out for everyone. I was truly blessed and very grateful to everyone for loving me just like their own child.

My dream is to write songs locally or nationally for a singer or group. But for now, I'd rather have a family enjoy them. Songs, poems, prayers, and testimonials have been placed on my heart by God, and I want to share them with you. Songs are written with the potential of becoming a great song. There is a message or story to be sang in character with people that you are comfortable with. Sunday's Best is a television talent show where my idea came from. Some of the judges said to the contestants that they "should record that song." To me, that was the start from amateur to professional. My tunes are mine alone. Establishing your own tunes will certainly make a song your song. Therefore, I wish everyone success!

There are two types of singers to me: there is the amateur/impersonator and there is the professional—with your God-given talents to sing and to be creative will make you original. By duplicating or impersonating someone else, the style of singing is a copycat to the original.

Real-life experiences are rooted in my songs, poems, prayers, and testimonials. Testimonials are my understanding of how I see my God. Each song and poem is based on my understanding; with my understanding, songs or poems are born. It is my hope that this book will entice readers to read the Bible or to stay in the Word; within this book is mentioned first my reasoning for the title according to Jesus's name. In addition, I am adding a biblical truth and answer frequently asked questionnaire (parts 1 and 2). Answer sheet, answers, and references are provided for your convenience. Materials covered within these pages stretch from Genesis to Revelation. The Bible used as reference is the Zondervan NIV (New International Version) Study Bible. The questionnaires within this book have questions that a Christian should know. Knowing about your neighbor's faith gains you respect and understanding.

To fight against sin, we must arm ourselves with truth, knowledge, and faith. Families are reminded of the fun that it is among themselves in quizzing each other. Still, there are many questions and answers not mentioned, but the pursuit in a family setting keeps us praising God. Everything that is written within this book is led by the Spirit; every home should possess the skill of reading. When you read, songs, poems, testimonials, and prayers may take on different interpretations according to each of us being unique. This is the beauty that I hope you may find within this book. Just don't forget, prayer is the most important phase of praising and worshiping. From your own relationship with God, prayer should be in your own words and not mine. Once again, be original (sincere) with prayer in your relationship with God.

There are many small singing groups in the world. Many of them start off with a few songs, until they find a writer that is tailor-made for their style of singing. I hope and pray that the songs mentioned will empower them to sing religious material. If anyone is singing my songs professionally, I reserve the rights to demand compensation for my work.

Legal representation will ensure that all parties enter into agreements fulfilling a partnership. I also reserve the rights to sell ownership of any song written by me once all parties agree to terms. Based on the successfulness of my first transcript, I may do another since I have written over 130 songs; only half will be in the two potential books. The songs not mentioned will be available to the individuals that have sung them professionally. Therefore, my dreams would be fulfilled. At this time, this is my intention, and my song count keeps rising until my God will call me to his home.

After the chapter "Conclusion" is "Special Addition," giving details to what happened to me as a formal correctional officer. The songs and testimonials are the most precious to me under "Special Addition." I can clearly say, "When I write a poem or song, I'm at peace, and my spirit is in a good place." When two or more good hearts pray for the Spirit to enter church, only to the righteous can it be felt. That is a partnership that leads to a congregation. Let us praise and worship God together for the whole world to enjoy.

Just Because

Testimonial

What does the name Jesus Christ mean to me?
My answer lies in his name.
My book title can best sum up the love that I have for my Lord.
Let us examine his name together.

First name

J   is for the "justice (law and order) that our Lord will bring."
E   is for "everyone who believes in his name."
S   is the "sacrifice that was made for you and me."
U   is for "us as a reminder to whom he died for."
S   again is for "Savior, who signifies that the ransom has been paid."

Last name

C   is for "Christmas, a holiday for gifts and praising his name."
H   is for the "hell that you will go to if not saved."
R   is for the "right to choose to be good or bad."
I   is for "his name Immanuel, which means God 'was with us as a man.'"
S   is for the "signs of prophecy that will follow until the end of days is near."
T   is for the "trials and tribulations to test one's faith in him."

Comments

Above are just a few meanings associated to his name. The love that I have for my Lord and Savior in my heart is "just because." But to love our Lord, you must put your love in action toward his people. Showing our fellow man human kindness is our greatest act of love for our Father in heaven.

Loving one another brings us closer to God, as it was designed to be from the beginning.

What does the name Jesus Christ mean to you?

The following pages are filled with songs, testimonials, prayers, poems, and questions. I hope that everyone will enjoy as I did while working for my Lord. Many distractions were put before me to do something else, but my heart wouldn't allow it because of the task put before me by my God.

I'm Sorry

Testimonial

There are times that we trespass against one another and forget to apologize to that person first before asking the Lord to forgive us.

We are eager to apologize to the Lord first and may never set things right against the one who suffered.

The words "I'm sorry" are used too often without sincerity.

In a bar, when someone steps on your feet and you'll say "I'm sorry," usually a fight may start.

This is because the atmosphere is sinful.

In church, when someone steps on your feet and you'll say "I'm sorry," usually a kind word is exchanged.

The atmosphere is different between church and a bar.

If love is in your spirit, then your spirit will guide you from harm.

If evil is in a person's spirit, then trouble usually follows.

The choice is yours for the making.

My choice is easy; I'd rather stay out of those bars.

I have seen the evil nature of a person in church trespassing against another.

Through prayer, we are united once again with one goal in mind.

This goal is praising and glorifying our Lord and Savior.

Many wars could have been prevented if handled correctly.

Don't try to force your ideas on another; the tongue has set off many wars.

Innocents have perished from another person's foolish differences.

I just hope this testimony is helpful to anyone with the courage to want to do good.

Trouble is easy to find and hard to get out of.

The words "I'm sorry" may not be enough.

A hug or a handshake showing sincerity goes a long way.

God Is God

Testimonial

How many of us believe that God is perfect?

There are many of us who believe this.

For me, I also believe this if not comparing to man-made objects. But there is a word above perfect; the word is God. Perfect is a word in which we humanize God and elevate our own accomplishments in man-made objects; in the beginning was God, not perfect God. Therefore, God stands alone over perfect and has no equal. A diamond can be made perfect, flawless according to man's standards.

Does the diamond become godly? No! Perfect is a word that we use to describe God. We make use of this word for our own benefit and not reserving it for spiritual meaning only. God is God according to my own understanding; we often hear the phrase "We serve a perfect God." Once you have experienced God for yourself, your meaning may change. Genesis 1 (the Beginning) begins with "God created" and "God said." The word perfect is used too often by man toward striving to perfection in the making of an object. Not spiritually! Jesus is above perfect, due to not having to strive toward perfection. Jesus is godly. Perfect is referred to God in the Old Testament, as spiritual maturity or completeness.

Mary's conception was not natural; she was not touched by man. Before she and Joseph came together, she was found to be with child by the Holy Spirit. This is a godly act. No sin can rest in the Holy Spirit; therefore, Jesus is sinless. Matthew 1:18 supports that Mary was with child before marriage to Joseph; we serve a God who is God Almighty. My existence and your existence are owed to God. Through the grace of God, all creation started! God is alone. Don't be confused when you read that God's word started creation. Later, the Word became Jesus in the flesh. In Matthew 1:23, Immanuel means "God with us." God (Father), the Son (Jesus, Lord), and the Holy Spirit (Holy Ghost, Comforter) are one. God is God! In Exodus 3:13–14, Moses said to God, "If asked, what name to give to his people." God said to Moses, "I am who I am." "I am" is God's first name, "who" is his middle name, and "I am" again is the last of God's name. The phrase "we serve a perfect God" means we serve a perfect title. The word God is a title to some people, not a name. Moses gave the Israelites the name given to him by God. "I am who I am" means God is God. "God is God" means "I am who I am." "I am who I am" reverts back before creation, and there was only God. When asked, does your God have a name? Your answer is yes. My answer is God is God. Jesus is Lord now; in order to get to the Father, you must go through him. Only the word of God will determine if we are heaven bound, and that is Jesus. This is why Christians follow Christ Jesus. Down below are words and their meanings to help you to understand clearly how I see God.

God—the supreme or ultimate reality

Perfect—being entirely without fault, flawless

Good—honorable

Fair—marked by impartiality and honesty

Today, we as human beings are using the bottom three for our own convenience. Only with the bottom two can we strive toward perfection, but still we fall short. I must say, even though I'm not perfect, I am worthy in my God's eyes. As my experiences in life grew with our Lord, my understanding changed with time. Jesus gave examples of character for his followers to strive for. I have heard phrases such as our "God is fair," "God is good all the time," and "We serve a perfect God." To me, I am serving a God who is "God Almighty." The word almighty describes the impossible and the unnatural; is your God fair, good, perfect, or something else? Which God are you serving? God has many names and names proclaimed from many people. No one in my mind can attest another person is wrong about their God. Never criticize another person about their beliefs and denomination. This is the only advice that my God has placed in my spirit to share with anyone seeking God. I am no preacher or deacon; my songs and poems are based on my understanding. If you persist in using the word perfect, I do not have a problem with that. I just think that fair, good, and perfect are characters of God. There are other words describing God's character, like holy, pure, righteous, and just. It is important never to separate the holiness of God from the love of God. The Holman QuickSource Bible Dictionary gives the knowledge, nature, and character of God.

Who Is Satan?

Testimonial

It is not wise to underestimate Satan; he was God's first angel. Satan has the power of notion and yields his power with lies and deceit without reservation; with deadly purpose, he will attack you indirectly, which means you may never see him coming. He has no love for man and is jealous of our favor with God. If you think you are above his approach, then he has you, and you are not aware of it.

Above his approach means that you are flawless, and according to my under standing, you are perfect! As an adversary of God, he will never weary due to his time here on earth is short. Satan is never your friend and will fail you in the end.

You must seek to stomp out his head when it arises.

If you are naive to his existence or too young to know, he will strike without hesitation. This is when we underestimate him. Pay heed to this warning be cause Satan is listening to win another soul for his hell.

Have You Taken Jesus to Trial?

Jesus Christ
Defendant

v.

The World
Society

Docket Number
AT-1234-06-5678-2-2

Date: June 6, AD 30
Evidence: The Bible (Zondervan NIV Study Bible)

Testimonial

Court is now in session.

Listen, have you heard that Pilate found no basis for a charge against Jesus? The chief priests and the crowd insisted that he's stirring up the people by his teachings all over Judea. Jesus was asked if he was a Galilean; the answer was yes. Therefore, Jesus fell under Herod's jurisdiction, and Pilate sent him away to be judged. Herod sent Jesus back because he could find no basis for the charges against him. Instead of releasing Jesus, one voice cried out, "Away with this man! Release Barabbas to us!" Barabbas had been thrown into prison for an insurrection in the city and for murder. Pilate appealed to the people again in wanting to release Jesus. But they kept shouting, "Crucify him!" Two other men, both criminals, were led out along with Jesus to be crucified. Jesus said, "Father, forgive them, for they do not know what they are doing." One of the criminals acknowledged Jesus being punished unjustly and asked Jesus to remember him in his kingdom. Jesus said, "I tell you the truth. Today, you will be with me in paradise."

In my last two statements, I'll say this, "Jesus put aside his pain and suffering and to welcome this man (a criminal) into his kingdom." The court system has been given the power by the people to judge and to execute sentencing on earth. Jesus has the power to judge being granted to him by his Father. All authority in heaven and on earth has been given to him after his resurrection.

Comments
(Thought)

On the cross, any other man would have been focused on themselves, but not our Lord and Savior. The evidence is clear to me that he is able to take any plea for mercy, forgiveness, and confessions. No matter what you are going through, our Lord is always able to the very end of age (time). Jesus was crucified as a result of a trial finding him guilty. On that day, the world (society) sentenced Jesus. Everyone must read the evidence for themselves and determine the outcome for themselves. Each of us must ask, is Jesus my Lord and Savior? As part of that society that has passed, we are equally blamed just as being there for the crucifixion. Therefore, when Jesus asked his father to forgive them, it was for the past, present, and future. If you have never taken anyone to court, or maybe you have not read the Bible for yourself, don't rely on someone else's interpretation; they can't save you. Regardless, Jesus was innocent but still had to die as prophesied. If your verdict is Jesus was not guilty of anything, then you are surely to die. On the other hand, if your verdict is guilty, then you are surely to live in his kingdom. Jesus is guilty for being our Lord and Savior; to pay the price for our sins and salvation, he had to be sinless. Trials and tribulations are essential (inherent) to earn our place in God's kingdom. Jesus was tested for the world to see, and he went through some things for us to have salvation. Jesus became the first martyr for mankind in my mind.

Conclusion

Closing arguments!

My evidences are outlined in Luke 22:66 through 23:43 and Matthew 28:18–20. Please read for your own interpretation and understanding.

The above docket number and date are fictitious. The testimonial is my understanding and may not sit well with others.

Jesus lost the case in the human world. But in the spiritual world, he won for you and me. His eternal love for mankind outweighed his worldly love and is truly a testament for all seers and doers of his name. This is why we say "Jesus has never lost a case." For the greater good, we now have the means to eternal life. When asked, "Have you tried Jesus?" this is your first trial for yourself; if you are convinced that he is your Lord and Savior, then prayer is your second option for your spirit to gain his supernatural power. Thank you, my God (the Father), for giving us Jesus.

Court is adjourned!

Godly Love

**Does everyone know what godly love is?
In comparison to man's love, man's love cannot compare.
Godly love started with creation, and then man's only job was to
    give our God praise.
After dominion was lost, Jesus as second "Adam" came later to
    restore what was lost.
For our salvation and eternal life, Jesus had to die as the sacrifice
    for the ransom to be paid in full.
*For the life of me, I cannot dismiss this feeling.
That many of us don't know
What godly, godly love is.
But I'm here to tell you all
That godly love must be the supreme love for mankind.
Please, everyone, do not take it likely!
Let it be shown by going to church
Let it be shown by helping one another
Let it be shown by praying for others than yourself.
That's what godly love must be.
If some of you all didn't get that
Just maybe no storm has visited you yet.
Not yet—I say to you!
Just you wait!

In the midst of everything
Some of us is still riding with the devil.
That's a ride that will be ending, ending very soon.
Just you wait!
With godly love, we as God's people have choices to be made.
The choices are to die twice for hell
Or to die once to claim the prize for heaven.
That's what godly love is to me.
**I hope now that many of us will be making a change.
From freedom of choice, our God trusts that we will make the
    best decision according to the life that we have lived.
By saying that maybe your future is heaven bound.
My brethren, choose well!
May the Lord keep you from the eminent dangers of this world.
There is no doubt in my mind
That John 3:16 reflects the full meaning of godly love.
And we as mankind are short-lived
But by having enough love and faith in our heart and soul
We have enough time to choose heaven
Through the name of Jesus.

Comments

The asterisk (*) is the start of singing.

Double asterisk (**) is testimony only. The prize is eternal life granted by Jesus. Heaven is the final resting place for those chosen for God's house, which is heaven. To me, the meaning of godly love is mentioned in John 3:16–18.

Abraham was the only man on earth that was tested to sacrifice his son (Isaac).

His decision stayed obedient to God. He was eventually stopped by God, and a ram was replaced as a burnt offering. Genesis 22:1–18 is the reference for my understanding.

Mary Magdalene's Remembrance of "Jesus" in the Grave

Song/Prayer

Oh, heavenly Father, have mercy for the Son of Man.
After the crucifixion, they laid our "Jesus" to rest.
(Choir) On the first day in the grave
Oh, my God, our Father, what is going on?
Is Jesus's work on earth finished, please, my Lord, give him
The power to get up from there?
(Choir) On the second day in the grave
Oh, my Lord, why is the Son of Man still there?
From a dream that night, I can hear "Satan" and "death"
Celebrating, shouting, "Victory at last over Jesus."
(Choir) But on the third day in the grave
Their victory was cut short.
There was a loud thunder, a sound that something was about
to happen.
So that morning, we visited the grave site where they laid my
Jesus to rest.
I could see that the stone and guards were gone.
As I entered the tomb, no Jesus was in sight.
While wondering about this, two men in clothes that gleamed
Like lightning stood beside us.

We were frightened at first, but the men's final words were "He
　　is not here."
(Choir) Oh, my God, your son has risen. The grave on earth had
　　no power over him.
Jesus was not the same man that I knew.
The Son of Man was no more, but the Son of God had risen
(Choir) Oh, my Lord, what is the meaning of all this?
The meaning was Jesus and a change was here.
So beware Satan and behold the Word of God!
Jesus is the word and answer for our salvation.
(Choir) Through Jesus, the means for eternal life is upon us.
Oh, thank you, heavenly Father, your son lives beyond the grave.
Amen!

Comments

This prayer was a song at first; it was put in my spirit from a dream
that I had. Therefore, be careful when digging a grave for someone,
you may need to dig two. Figuratively speaking, Satan dug a grave
for Jesus and fell in it himself. Also, there were three people that
Jesus restored to life. Are the three days in the grave and three
people that Jesus restored to life truly coincidental? Did Jesus's
work on earth speak for him? My answer would be yes. What
would you're answer be for the three days in the grave?

Luke 24:6–7 clearly gives reference to the three days. Jesus had
predicted his death and resurrection on a number of occasions
while in Galilee. Different authors of the Bible put different people
at the time of the resurrection. Mary Magdalene is named first in
most of the lists of women and was the first to see the risen Christ.

I'm a Child: The Boy Jesus at the Temple

(Two lead singers)

Song/Testimonial

(Lead 1) At a young age, Jesus stood up for his Father.
I can recall that he was twelve years old.
Many questions that he did ask
And many questions that were put to him
And he never abandoned the truth.
The truth is
He is the Son of God.
Just before puberty, we can all choose the Lord.
Or we can all choose the devil.
To remain obedient, there are tests
That we must endure to stay focused on our Lord and Savior.
Here's one question!
Is your faith strong enough regardless of your age
To follow Jesus? If yes is your answer.
Then remain focused on Jesus!
Time is a factor to be considered because we do not know
How long our life expectancy is.
All young people, choose well!

Satan is waiting
To win another soul for his hell.
Everyone is young to somebody.
Pause! What am I?
I'm just a young child of God.
Trying to praise my Lord.
And we all can choose heaven
Or we all can choose hell.
How … would you … choose?
(Lead 2) For me, I chose heaven.
Please, everyone
Praise God, the Son, and the Holy Spirit.
As a child, I thought like a child.
Now that I am all grown-up
I must put away those childly things.
But I'm praising my God
(Leads 1 and 2) Hallelujah! Right now! (repeat)
We are choosing our Lord and Savior.
*Look up!
Yes, Jesus, it is you that we have chosen
And not mankind recruited by Satan.

Comments

"The Boy Jesus at the Temple" is found in Luke 2:41–51. Lead 1 is a young adolescent child. Lead 2 is a young man or woman. Since the title is centered on a young adolescent child, it is more fitting that the child has more to say. The asterisk (*) is for direction only.

Noah's Next-Door Neighbors

Song

Listen, everyone, a man next door is building an ark.
He says God has spoken to him, saying, "Be prepared for a flood
 like no other."
Everyone is laughing at him, but still he's continuing to build
 an ark.
Finally, the rain comes, with no ending in sight.
The water seems to keep on rising.
My Lord, it isn't funny anymore.
Oh, my Lord, they should have listened.
I can hear the rain falling down with no end in sight.
The water keeps on rising and rising.
Eventually, water did cover the whole earth.
Noah's ark was floating like at sea.
My parents and me did board the ark.
Others knocked on the ark that Noah built, but he did not open.
Instead of crying out to Noah to open, they should have listened
 to a man of God.
Momma and Daddy, why won't he let them in?
Could it be because that there was not enough room in the ark?
They should have listened and built their own ark.
Voices of the old and young crying out, but it was too late!
From the Bible, God established his covenant with Noah.

As a reminder to God and the earth, a rainbow will be the sign
    of the covenant
for all living creatures to see.
Momma and Daddy, are they going to listen next time?
(Chorus) Only time will tell, my son.
Time will tell on us all.

Comments

If you can recall, everyone did perish from the flood except the people aboard the ark. This song is intended for a young person to sing after reading about Noah. The parents of the young person are present as this song is being sung. The choir is the parents. The next-door neighbors are the parents and grown son that boarded Noah's ark. Noah could not open the doors to the ark because God sealed them shut.

In the *World Book Encyclopedia*, Noah warned people for 120 years that the flood was coming. Deluge or great flood was what it is referred to as.

OMG (Oh, Mighty God)

*Oh, heavenly Father
While looking back over the years
Tragedies and disasters have struck.
Almost and nearly could have been me
And all I could say was "Oh, my God."
From the news yesterday
A devastating storm flooded a small town.
Mudslides were created
And cars and homes were damaged
And death took its toll on the townspeople.
And all I could say was "Oh, my God."
It is times like this
That I could be running out of time.
And I'll say, "Oh, my God."
For now, everything is quiet and calm
And OMG is not called.
Now what is wrong with this, may I ask?
We only acknowledge God through tragedies and disasters.
Oh, heavenly Father
Please forgive me
*For using your name in vain.
**It is silly because we are accrediting our God to something bad.

When your child comes home with straight As
When you find out that your child has been born again
Or you find out that your wife is going to have twins
Those are the times to say "oh, my God."
Since my God is almighty
Instead of saying, "Oh, my God," "Oh, mighty God" is more accurate.
Now with the new saying
"Oh, mighty God" is for everyone
And may "Oh, my God" be forgiven
On my behalf for speaking the words, my Lord.
I must admit that it would be hard to shake
That old saying "Oh, my God"
And start using "Oh, Mighty God"
So right now, Lord, I'm giving you all the glory.
Still, "Oh, my God" may come out my mouth
But "Oh, mighty God" will be in my heart
Giving you, my Lord, all the praises and honors
For being "Oh, mighty God" for us all!

Comments

Single asterisk (*) is song and prayer. Double asterisk (**) is for testimony. We must remind ourselves that God is always in control. Words sometimes used by mouth do not reflect our hearts always. This is why our Lord reads the hearts of all men.

Bedtime Song

Poem/Song/Prayer

My Lord
Before I lay down to sleep, I pray to God for my soul to keep
I look toward heaven for Jesus to bless me with peace.
Now is the time to ask God for forgiveness and to heed
his sovereignty.
Never will I change my position on sin.
Never will I give up on Jesus, not now or then.
While drifting to sleep, my mind is calm
And the God I serve watches over me.
I pray each night that my work on earth is pleasing to my God
And for a place in his kingdom for me.
On each and every morning that I rise
I know it couldn't have happened without our Father above
the skies.
I cherish each morning like it's new for the first time
And may Jesus find favor in me to shine.
Lord, I look to you on every hour of every day.
While I sleep, my divine safety rests in your hands
Who's not to say?
There is a promise upon one day that I'll see the promise land.
I'll await Jesus's return and look toward the clouds.

I'm hoping to remain on the right hand of his might
And watch Satan fall from the fight.
Mother Earth is the promise land
And only the righteous will inherit the space above the sand.
Amen!

Let Us Pray

Song/Prayer

Lord
Very often, when circumstances happen without reasoning
We as people find ourselves in limbo.
There is a time when our faith is questionable
And our lack of understanding may be lost.
The question remains as to what we as people must do.
(Ch) Let us pray!
Some of us pray for rain
Some of us pray for our finances to get better
Some of us pray for a stronger relationship with our God.
(Ch) Let us pray!
Amen to that, "let us pray" is a good choice.
When there are good days
When there are bad days
When there is sickness and the doctor has given up on you.
(Ch) Let us pray!
It is said that "Man born from woman after a few days
Will know trouble."
To me, my thoughts are "we will always fall short."
This is why I must pray.
(Ch) Let us pray!
Father God, hear this prayer

I am at your mercy
Please heal me when I am sick
Please comfort me when I am sad
Please help me to grow stronger in my relationship with you.
Through Jesus's name
Amen!

J-O-B

Song

Does everyone have J-O-B?
(Ch) Yes!
No! I don't mean a job.
Do you have Jesus on board in your life?
If not, what are you doing about it?
Life is too short to put it on hold.
(Ch) Well
Some of us are thinking that later is better.
Believe me when I say this, "Later might be tonight."
(Ch) What you say!
Think about it, tonight or tomorrow is not promised to anyone.
Ask yourself this question, "Do I have J-O-B?"
If your answer is yes, then act like it.
Don't act a certain way after leaving church.
Church people act the same way all the time.
It's because they have J-O-B.
(Ch) Well, well, well!
Listen, when you and me act a certain way
It's not because that we are hypocrites
It's because we have fallen short.
(Ch) Repent!
That's right!

We must repent.
J-O-B is for everyone.
(Ch) We have J-O-B!
I have J-O-B!
Jesus is an equal opportunity lord.
He doesn't cater just to the rich.
Redemption is to wipe your slate clean,
(Ch) We have J-O-B!
Say it again!
(Ch) We have J-O-B!
With J-O-B comes everlasting life.
How do I know this?
Because our Bible tells me so.
Look to your neighbor
And ask, "Do you have J-O-B?"
Yes, yes, J-O-B is for everyone.
(Ch) Jesus, we are on board
With your yes, Lord, your Spirit
And your yes, Lord, Your holy name.

Jesus Commands Death to Free Lazarus's Requirement

(Two lead singers; one is Jesus)

Song

> (Lead 1) Lazarus, my faithful servant, come forth
> It is I who command thee.
> (Lead 2) But death has a hold on me.
> It has been four days
> And my grave is dark and cold.
> (Lead 1) Lazarus, believe in me!
> Death, release my obedient servant!
> It is I (Jesus) that command thee.
> I am the Son of the ever-living God.
> Come, Lazarus! Come now, my servant!
> Come to the sound of my voice.
> (Lead 2) My Lord! I am … coming.
> Lord, your voice is so loud and clear.
> Although my clothes are not fresh
> I can see some light as I make my way to the entrance.
> (Lead 1) Remove your burial clothes
> Death has to let you go.
> (Lead 2) Yes, Lord!
> It is good to be among the living again.

Thank *you*, Lord!
(Lead 1) Lazarus, go forth among the unbelievers.
To renew their faith in me.
(Lead 2) But, Lord, how would I be received?
(Lead 1) Your presence is a testimony to my Father's glory
That same glory is passed down to me.
(Lead 2) Yes, my Lord
I will obey.
(Lead 1) Yes, my servant, I know you will.
(Lead 2) "Je … sus," how I love the sound
Your voice was all that I could hear
Calling my name.
Yes, yes!
I love the voice and sound of "Je … sus."
Does everyone hear what I am saying?
Jesus not only woke me from my living sleep
But also from my gravely sleep.
Oh, yes, how I love the sound of Jesus.
Say his name (repeat)
One more time.
"Je … sus!"

Comments

The death of Lazarus is found in John 11. John 11:25 is what Jesus said. The three people that Jesus raised from the grave can only die once. To die again, they are with Jesus to the end of time, which means to me, when the books are open, their names are recorded for heaven. Judgment will only be once. Your view may be different from mine, and that is all right. Before Jesus's death on the cross, the thief asked him to remember him in his kingdom; judgment was at that moment, according to my understanding. Judgment was before death, because the power was given to Jesus. All of the above acts took place on earth. After Jesus's resurrection, all authority in heaven and on earth has been given to him. The Father, the Son, and the Holy Spirit are a team; if you run a relay race and pass on the baton, you are looked at as one. In the spiritual world, this is true also.

Lazarus's Response to "Jesus" Raising the Dead

Song

Hey, out there! I'm alive!
I'm happy to be seeing you all
For you all are seeing me.
My last four days I must say
That I was not a part of the living world.
You see, I was sleeping in my grave.
But Jesus woke me up that day!
(Ch) what you say!
I was wrapped from head to toe
In my burial clothes.
But Jesus called my name
Pause!
Death had to ... let me go.
(Ch) Say what!
Yes, if you think that you have it bad
Try sleeping in a dark and cold grave.
Nothing is worse than that
For I am here to tell you.
(Ch) Who called your name?
It was Jesus

I heard a voice in darkness calling my name.
Can you see why I'm so happy?
(Ch) My Lord! Yes, Jesus! Hallelujah!
I can see that some of you all are happy also.
My presence is a testimony to God's glory. Thank you...Jesus!

Comment

"Jesus raises Lazarus from the dead" is found in John 11:38–44.

Mother Always Said

Song

Just before my mother had passed away
What she said was, "Son, always remember."
Here's a few and final words
Left from her
And from on her dying bed.
"Son, before your eyes are closed for sleep
Be sure to pray to Jesus
To bank a prayer for a restful sleep."
(Ch) Mother always said!
"Brush your teeth while they are still in your head.
Take a bath just before bed.
Be sure to wash within and behind those ears
To hear better to what is being said."
(Ch) Mother always said!
"Never take thy God for granted
To always honor and obey his Ten Commandments."
Then she closed her eyes like in sleep.
Never to awake until judgment is passed
On her and later on down to me.
(Ch) This is what was said from Mother to me.
"Always remember to pray
Just before bed

To honor and obey the Ten Commandments
Because one more prayer may have been needed
To get you into heaven
And not Satan's hell for the dead."
(Ch) Everyone, always listen to your mother.
Her words of wisdom are passed on from love
And never from hate
Leading up to her last dying breath.
These are a few and her last words
While on earth, this was what my mother always said.

Comments

In most cases, mothers are the first bond of a child. Some mothers die giving birth and may have known the risks. But their love was greater for their child, than for themselves.

As long as I can remember, Momma will always be with me.

Mothers will put themselves in harm's way to save a child. But Jesus was the sacrificial Lamb for the whole world. The world saw Jesus die; now we must always remember the wisdom and believe that he will come again.

FLAME (Father God Loves All Men Eternally)

Song

Within many of us, there exists a FLAME from our God.
And in return, our Father God expects us to love him.
Not by demand or by force!
But by choice!
(Ch) How do we know this?
He gave his only begotten Son
That whomever believes in him will not perish
And will have ever lasting life.
(Ch) How do we know that?
From reading our Bible for ourselves.
(Ch) Does the FLAME burn in everyone?
Only you can answer that question.
For me, my answer is yes.
*Look up!
Father, keep your FLAME burning…within me.
Don't let me fall from your grace, O Lord.
(Ch) Father, keep the FLAME burning
In all of us.
Stand up, everyone; let God know that his FLAME burns
within you.

Shout if you must, clap if you must
But don't sit there any longer in silence.
(Ch) Father God, your FLAME burns within me!
We are your followers, my Lord.
And we will follow you, follow until the end.
Yes, yes, toward eternality!
(Ch) Your FLAME is a burning ray, Lord, within me!
Please, everyone, don't let Satan
Extinguish your FLAME.
Second death is hellfire
Meaning no more spirit
And that you are gone forever.
Keep the flame burning and live eternally!
(Ch) Oh, Lord, your FLAME burns hot in all of our hearts.
*Look into the audience!
Please, everyone, keep the FIRE renewed
By adding air and fuel
To your FLAME.
I wouldn't want nothing else
But eternal life for you
And for the ones that are already gone.
(Ch) Keep your FLAME burning within me, Lord!
Never let Satan extinguish my FLAME, Lord *Jesus.*
My FLAME is fueled by my trials and tribulations.
And may Jesus stay strong within each and every one
That truly believe that he will come again.

Comments

All flames of a fire must be maintained, or it would eventually go out. A strong spirit means that you have added to the fire. By doing so, your FIRE or FLAME burns bright for the whole world to see. Air and fuel are your trials and tribulations. The sparks from the FLAME ignite singing, various artists, doctors, lawyers, and faithful servants. The asterisk (*) is for direction only. FIRE from above means Father God is real eternally.

The Cross

Question: Why is the cross important to a Christian?

Cross, Crucifixion: Method the Romans used to execute Jesus Christ. The most painful and degrading form of capital punishment in the ancient world, the cross became the means by which Jesus became the atoning sacrifice for the sins of all mankind. It also became a symbol for the sacrifice of self in discipleship (Rom. 12:1) and for the death of self to the world (Mark 8:34).

For Paul, the "word of the cross" (Cor. 1:18 NASB) is the heart of the gospel, and the preaching of the cross is the soul of the church's mission. "Christ crucified" (Cor. 1:23, cp. 2:2; Gal. 3:1) is more than the basis of our salvation; the cross was the central event in history, the one moment that demonstrated God's control of and involvement in human history.

Jesus himself established the primary figurative interpretation of the cross as a call to complete surrender to God. He used it five times as a symbol of true discipleship in terms of self-denial, taking up one's cross, and following Jesus (Mark 8:34, 10:38; Matt. 16:24; Luke 9:23, 14:27).

Closely connected to this is Paul's symbol of the crucified life. Conversion means the individual "no longer live(s)" but is replaced by Christ and faith in him (Gal. 2:20). Self-centered desires are nailed to the cross (Gal. 5:24), and worldly interests are dead (Gal. 6:14). The Christian paradox is that death is the path to life.

Comments

Reference is the *Holman QuickSource Bible Dictionary*, while holding Bible study with Jehovah's Witnesses, that question was asked frequently. To all fellow Christians, examine the reference for yourself and remember that you maybe called to defend our Lord and Savior for yourself. Jesus doesn't need defending from people that don't believe in him. As an individual, each of us is tasked with choosing to believe or not.

Jesus Bears the Cross

Song

With all eyes closed!
While thinking back and looking up and seeing Jesus on the cross.
(Ch) Why are y'all nailing, my Lord, to that cross?
(Ch) He was tried and found guilty of nothing.
Lord … Lord, I'm at my lowest today.
My explanation for the crucifixion is not too clear.
But Father (God), all I can see is my sweet Jesus up on that cross.
Nothing around me seems to matter, but the reasons are very
    clear to the question of "Why you're on that cross?"
(Ch) Lord, Lord, oh, Lord!
I'm picturing myself before you on that cross; nothing seems to
    matter but the why.
No matter how low that I feel, I can only look up and see
Your pain and suffering on that cross.
So I tell myself, no matter what I am going through, someone
    else is suffering worse than me.
You all may see, the pain and suffering really remind us why we
    need Jesus.
Lord, I must admit there are times that I'll forget about
You when things are good.
But right now, Lord, I'm praising you for the good and the bad.

In my spirit, I must remind myself to give thanks through the good and the bad.

The bad is not bad at all but a test to draw me closer to You, oh, God.

Lord, I am asking you for your forgiveness.

Shower me with your blessings, one after another.

(Ch) Lord, oh, Lord! Lord,

forgive me for a moment for focusing on me.

But I know it's not about me, it's all about you, my God!

I know in my heart if you can take the abuse that the people at your feet showed.

I can take whatever life throws at me. Oh, God, please forgive me for all my sins.

There's no one that I know on this earth that would have asked his Father to forgive them, because they know not what they do.

(Ch) What a powerful God we serve!

I'm telling you, I will serve him ... serve him until the end.

Right now, I got to praise him and I got to get it out.

I got to praise, and I got to get it out; I got to praise ... Jesus!

Clap your hands, stomp your feet, and shout for the Lord like it's your last day on earth.

That day was Jesus's last day as the Son of Man.

Today or tomorrow may be my last, yes, my last day or yours.

(Ch) Give him the glory! (repeat)

Give Je ... sus ... all the glory.

Comments

I would like to introduce "Seven Words from the Cross."

In preparation to leave this earth as being a sacrificial Lamb for the world to see, Jesus endured the agony for the world. Here are statements that Jesus made during the six agonizing hours of his crucifixion: (1) He asked forgiveness for those who crucified him (Luke 23:34). (2) He promised the penitent thief he would meet the Lord in paradise that very day (Luke 23:43). (3) He made provision for the care of his mother by the apostle John (John

19:26–27). (4) His fourth statement was a cry of isolation, quoting Psalm 22:1 (Mark 15:34). (5) His physical agony was expressed in the fifth statement, when he acknowledged his thirst (John 19:28). (6) "It is finished" (John 19:30) was a cry of victory, not defeat. (7) Jesus quoted Psalm 31:5 as he committed his spirit to God (Luke 23:46). This is the reason for the word why in the song above. "Seven Words from the Cross" is found in *the Holman QuickSource Bible Dictionary*. Jesus's mission here on earth was completed, and he returned back to the Father. The makeup of God to a Christian is the Father, the Son, and the Holy Spirit/Ghost.

Borrowed Time

Song

For those of you
That are afraid of death
Take a good look at the deceased
Being laid out and due for a long rest.
He/she maybe should have been dead a long time ago.
But our God saw fit to take this person among the living.
Now that he has released this person from the living.
There is no more pain or suffering
For now, he/she is waiting on Jesus.
Listen, being born one day
Is the same as one hundred years to our God.
Therefore, I am asking everyone
Don't weep too long for the deceased.
Dying is easy
It was living that was found to be hard.
Say a quick word or two before the body is committed to the ground.
Afterward, please be on your way
Because in the graveyard
There is no room for the living.
All the borrowed time has now come to an end.
And this person is in a good place
Awaiting Jesus's final decision of heaven, hopefully not hell!

This person lived loving our heavenly Father and his Son.
Now, in death, nothing has changed, I tell you.
All the borrowed time has expired, I say to friends and family.
Lay him/her down somewhere looking up
So he/she can see Jesus when he comes.
Right now, he/she says, "Goodbye, world"
Must keep appointment with Jesus.
I only ask that you bury him/her quickly
So later on, before our Lord and Savior to come one day.
May our God continue to bless
Each and every one attending and not attending.
On borrowed time, it was approved by our God
Now in death, he/she is set free upon second journey.
For loving Jesus, he/she loved him in life
And now, this person's love will carry over into death.
He/she thanked Jesus for a good life among the living. Among
the dead
Borrowed time is nowhere to be found.
This was his/her time to say farewell
"Farewell, world," this person's departure is not sad
But a happy one because he/she is now with Jesus.
Until the end!

Comments

Before you die, you can give voice with the assistance of someone sharing your views on life. Today, many people are creating recordings and videos, to convey their feelings on death, before actually dying. Their resume for life will be recorded for Jesus to decide heaven or hell. The book of life is where all resumes are kept and will be opened on judgment day by Jesus.

Thirty-Three Years

Song

On this earth
Our Lord and Savior graced us with his presence.
Give or take twelve thousand and forty-five days
He healed the lame, restored sight to the blind
Removed demons, and restored life to the dead.
Wait, just one minute!
That wasn't all that he did
Then he died up on that cross for you and me
Three days later, he was up with the Holy Spirit
With all power and authority given to him from God.
(Ch) Thirty-three years!
Jesus appeared thirteen times after his resurrection, according
    to Luke 24:15.
*(Ch) Yes, thirty-three long years!
What is a person supposed to do? I'll tell you
Give him praise because he was the only one
Only one worthy to die for our sins and salvation.
(Ch) Yes, thirty-three long years!
On that cross, victory was won.
Not defeat!
Yes, yes, my Lord!
This is why the cross has great meaning to a Christian

(Ch) Thirty-three years, I say!
Pause!
**(Look up)
Father God, your Son strengthens our beliefs.
In you
No one else could have paid the price for our salvation.
**(Face the audience)
Jesus accomplished everything that his Father has tasked him
    with then and now.
Will you stand and give him the thanks that he deserves
(Ch) Thirty-three years!
At night, just before you go to sleep, continue to thank
Jesus and the Father
By falling down on bended knee(s).
*(Ch) Thirty-three years!
Father God, your Son's words are like food put on the table.
Taking in his nourishment enables one's soul to be saved.
Jesus is the word…from God.
(Ch) Thirty-three long years!
Three hundred and ninety-six months may not have seemed long.
But it was enough time for our Lord to do our Master's will.
His tasks were completed here on earth.
It became time for Jesus to return back to the Father.
Judgment is the next time that he will appear.
So I say to everyone, "You better get ready!"
Ready or not, Jesus will be coming, coming very soon.

Comments

The asterisk (*) is the extended version from beginning to end. The double asterisk is for direction only.

Jesus's life here on earth was with purpose after God cast out Adam and Eve from the garden. Our God has a way of restoring what was lost (dominion), and the way to the Father is through Jesus. For many years, we hear different names for God, but there is only one name given to our Lord. The name is *Jesus.*

9-1-1

(Requirement: Two singers)

Song

Phone ringing!
(2) *Kneel down and wait until someone answers.
(1) "This is 9-1-1, what's the nature of your emergency?"
(2) "I need to speak to Jesus, please connect me."
(1) "Why?"
(2) "My spirit is broken, and I don't know how to fix it."
Fix me, Jesus; I'm calling on you, Lord!
Fix me, Jesus, in the name of the Father!
Fix me, Jesus; fix me, Lord!
Put me back together again, Lord, to do my Master's will
This is your humble servant asking you to fix me, Jesus
My heart is overwhelmed with your Holy Spirit.
I'm feeling your healing powers throughout my soul.
I'm rising to my feet, Lord; thank you, Jesus!
It was your power that made me whole again.
I am a living testimony.
Thank you, Lord!
Thank you, my Lord!
Incoming call!
(1) "This is 9-1-1; caller, please stay on the line."

(2) God is on the line giving me a place in his kingdom.
Thank you, Father, the Son, and the Holy Spirit.
Lord, keep me close to your bosom.
Protect me from the eminent dangers of this world.
Jesus has fixed me, and he can do the same for you.
(1) Just call him!
Just call on the name of the Lord.
(2) I'm glad I tried, Jesus.
Yes, yes!
I'm glad, and my soul is healed.
(1 and 2) Thank you, Jesus! Thank you, my Lord!

Comment

Asterisk (*) is for direction only.

Holy Day

Song/Testimonial

For we as being God-fearing people have always look
toward holidays.

Some holidays are not that significant to some people.

Some holidays give birth to a day that can be remembered.

But when Jesus comes again

Oh, my God

That day may be called a holy day.

Pause!

All the other holidays do come during seasons.

But our Lord Jesus will bring a season like no other

And all by himself.

Brethren, don't let that day catch you on the wrong side.

Be prepared to welcome Jesus when he comes.

As prophesied, our Lord will come like a thief in the night.

We can all be assured that he will set things right.

At this time, Satan has lost a long fight.

Pause!

There is no room for Satan in God's kingdom.

So, brethren, get on the right side.

The right side is Jesus.

All hopes and prayers are finally answered on that day.

That day may be called a holy day!

Let me tell you why it may be called a holy day.
That day will never end.
No more days of the week will come.
No more Sabbath day set aside for praising.
Holy day
Eden would have returned once again on earth.
Where every saved soul's job is to praise and worship
Our Father and the Son
As to if it was their last
But will be there first for eternity.
That's what a holy day is to me.
Oh, yes, when Jesus comes again, it will be a holy day.
This holy day will last
For eter…ni…ty!
Welcome back, Eden!

Comments

This song is a vision of things to come.

This vision gave way to my understanding and now placed in a song for those who have the same vision. Heaven is Eden being returned on earth where it all began.

Biblical Truth and Answers

Part 1

Frequently Asked Biblical Questions

(Answer sheet is provided.)

1. Question: In the beginning, what day man was created?

    Answer: a. Two b. Nine c. Six

2. Q: In the garden of Eden, what form did Satan appeared in?

    A: a. Goat b. Cow c. Serpent

3. Q: Who is not Noah's son?

    A: a. Shem b. Japheth c. Ham d. Seth

4. Q: How did God first appear to Moses?

    A: a. Burning bush b. rock c. ram d. light

5. Q: How many plagues did Moses bring upon Pharoah?

    A: a. 12 b. 10 c. 15 d. 7

6. Q: Which is the last book of Moses?

    A: a. Deuteronomy b. Numbers c. Leviticus

7. Q: Who betrayed Jesus?

    A: a. Simon b. Judas c. Iscariot d. Peter

8. Q: Where did Samson's strength come from while battling the Philistines?

    A: a. Mustache b. Beard c. Hair

9. Q: What did Samson use to kill a thousand men?

    A: a. Sword b. Spear c. Donkey's jawbone

10. Q: In the middle of the garden of Eden, what tree(s) was not permitted to be eaten from?

    A: a. Tree of good will b. Tree of life c. Tree of knowledge

11. Q: What was the covenant between God and Noah?

    A: a. Rainbow in the clouds b. Solar eclipse c. Fallen star

12. Q: In the Tower of Babel, what did God do to prevent the building of the tower?

    A: a. Bless his people b. Destroy the tower c. Confuse the language

13. Q: What was the last plague Moses brought upon Pharoah?

    A: a. Plague of Blood b. Plague on the Firstborn c. Plague of Boils

14. Q: Moses asked God what name to give the Israelites when they asked his name?

    A: a. Yahweh b. Jehovah c. I Am who I Am

15. In the beginning, God created Adam and____ .

    A: a. Steve b. Eve c. Dawn

16. Q: Who was Adam's first son?

    A: a. Abel b. Moses c. Cain

17. Q: What city did Lot flee to before the destruction of Sodom and Gomorrah?

    A: a. Zoar b. Joppa c. Damascus

18. Q: How old was Moses when he died?

    A: a. 90 b. 110 c. 120

19. Q: The Old Testament has _____ books.

    A: a. 37 b. 44 c. 39

20. Q: The New Testament has _____ books.

    A: a. 27 b. 37 c. 39

21. Q: What governor did Jesus stand before?

    A: a. Judas b. Barabbas c. Pilate

22. "The Lord is my shepherd, I shall not be in want" is the start of the Psalm.

    A: a. 22 b. 23 c. 25

23. Q: What book is after Psalms in the Bible?

    A: a. Proverbs b. Ecclesiastes c. Isaiah

24. Q: What book is before Revelation in the Bible?

    A: a. Hebrews b. Jude c. 2 Peter

25. Q: What year was Abram born?

    A: a. AD 2166 b. 2166 BC c. AD 2100

26. Q: In what year did Abram/Abraham die?

    A: a. 1991 BC b. AD 1800 c. AD 1991

27. Q: In what year was Moses born?

    A: a. AD 1915 b. 1526 BC c. 1105 BC

28. Q: In the Old Testament, what is the chronological order in which the world was started?

    A: a. Fall b. Babel c. creation d. Flood

29. Q: From the destruction of Sodom and Gomorrah, who looked back and became a pillar of salt?

    A: a. Lot's oldest daughter b. Lot's son c. Lot's wife

30. Q: In Genesis, who is the only female not birthed by woman?

    A: a. Rita b. Eve c. Nina

31. Q: In biblical history, what was the year after Babel?

    A: a. AD 2500 b. 2500 BC c. 0001 BC

32. The first five books of Jewish and Christian scriptures are often referred to as .

    A: a. Pentateuch b. Pentagram c. Pentecost

33. Q: What book is after Deuteronomy in the Bible?

    A: a. Judges b. Joshua c. Job

34. The story of David and Goliath is found in .

    A: a. 2 Samuel b. 1 Samuel c. 1 Kings

35. Q: What book is before Job?

    A: a. Psalm b. Jeremiah c. Esther

36. Q: Judah, Reuben, Gad, Asher, Naphtali, Manasseh, Simeon, Levi, Issachar, Zebulun, Joseph, and Benjamin are the twelve tribes of Israel found in Revelation, what is their sealed number?

    A: a. 14,000 b. 16,000 c. 12,000

37. Q: If you take the answer to question 36, what is the total of those who will be sealed?

    A: a. 144,000 b. 166,000 c. 180,000

38. Q: Which of the following names does not refer to God?

    A: a. Elohim b. El Shaddai c. El olam d. Nero

39. Q: How many times did Jesus appear after the resurrection?

    A: a. 4 b. 9 c. 13

40. Q: Who were the three people Jesus raised from death?

    A: a. Lazarus b. Herod c. Widow's son at Nain d. Jairus's daughter

41. Q: In Job's second test, who below is not his friend?

    A: a. Eliphaz b. Bildad c. Elihu d. Zophar

42. Q: In Job's first test, the angels came to present themselves before the Lord, who also came with them?

    A: a. Peter b. Satan c. Jesus

43. In Romans, righteousness from God comes through faith in Jesus Christ to all who believe.

    True or False

44. In Jeremiah, the word of the Lord came to say, "Before I formed you in the womb I knew you, before you were born I set you apart; I appointed you as a prophet to the nations."

    True or False

45. Q: Was Jesus a Prophet, Messiah, or Savior?

You must decide!

46. Q: This person was king of Salem and priest of God Most High. He met Abraham returning from the defeat of the kings and blessed him, and Abraham gave him a tenth of everything, who was this person?

A: a. Melchizedek b. Levi c. Ezekiel

47. Q: King Nebuchadnezzar was furious with three men and gave orders for these three men to be thrown into a blazing furnace, who were the three men?

A: a. Shadrach b. Issachar c. Abednego d. Meshach

48. Q: Which book of the Bible provides the rules for being a priest?

A: a. Numbers b. Leviticus c. Romans

49. Q: In Revelation, "The woman and the dragon," the women fled to the desert to a place prepared by God. How many days in the desert that she might be taken care of?

A: a. 120 b. 1,000 c. 1,260

50. In Revelation, an angel coming down from heaven will seize the dragon (i.e., Satan/devil) and bind him for years.

A: a. 500 b. 750 c. 1,000 d. 1,500

51. Q: In Genesis, the call of Abram, Abram took his wife Sarai,_____ ,_____ and they set out for the land of Canaan.

A: a. His young cousin b. His nephew Lot c. His uncle Lot

How did you do? Check your answers to find out. Top score is fifty. (These questions were prepared, researched, and written by Mr. Gregory Dixon.)

Biblical Truth and Answers

Part 1

Answer Sheet

1. _____
2. _____
3. _____
4. _____
5. _____
6. _____
7. _____
8. _____
9. _____
10. _____
11. _____
12. _____
13. _____
14. _____
15. _____
16. _____
17. _____
18. _____

19. _____

20. _____

21. _____

22. _____

23. _____

24. _____

25. _____

26. _____

27. _____

28. _____

29. _____

30. _____

31. _____

32. _____

33. _____

34. _____

35. _____

36. _____

37. _____

38. _____

39. _____

40. _____

41. _____

42. _____

43. _____

44. _____

45. _____

46. _____

47. _____

48. _____

49. _____

50. _____

51. _____

Biblical Truth and Answers

Part 1

Answers

Each question is worth two points except for question 45 and the bonus question. Ninety-nine and a half is the top score; if your faith is strong, a score of fifty may get you into heaven.

1. c
2. c
3. b
4. a
5. b
6. a
7. b, c
8. c
9. c
10. c
11. a
12. c
13. b
14. c
15. b

16. c

17. a

18. c

19. c

20. a

21. c

22. b

23. a

24. b

25. b

26. a

27. b

28. c, a, d, b

29. c

30. b

31. b

32. a

33. b

34. b

35. c

36. c

37. a

38. d

39. c

40. a, c, d

41. c

42. b

43. True

44. True

45. You must decide!

46. a

47. a c d

48. b

49. c

50. c

51. b

Biblical Truth and Answers

Part 1

References

Zondervan NIV study Bible

1. Gen. 1:26–31
2. Gen. 3
3. Gen. 6:10
4. Exod. 3
5. Exod. 7–11
6. Deut. Introduction
7. Matt. 26:14
8. Jdg. 16:17–19
9. Judg. 15:15–16
10. Gen. 2:9–17
11. Gen. 9:12–13
12. Gen. 10:6–7
13. Exod. 11
14. Exod. 3:14–15
15. Gen. 2:22–23
16. Gen. 4
17. Gen. 19:22–23

18. Deut. 34:7

19. Table of Contents

20. Table of Contents

21. Matt. 27:11

22. Ps. 23:1

23. Table of Contents

24. Table of Contents

25. Old Testament Chronology/Second Page

26. Old Testament Chronology/Second Page

27. Old Testament Chronology/Third Page

28. Old Testament Chronology/First Page

29. Gen. 19:26

30. Gen. 2:22

31. Old Testament Chronology/Second Page

32. Gen. Introduction

33. Tables of Contents

34. Isa. 17:1

35. Tables of Contents

36. Rev. 7:4-8

37. Rev. 7:5-8

38. Page 2032/Names of God

39. Resurrection Appearances Table in Luke/Page 1620

40. Isa. 11:1–44, Luke 7:11–15, Mark 5:22–24

41. Job 2:11

42. Job 1:6

43. Rom. 3:21–26

44. Jer. 1:4–5

45.

46. Heb. 7:1–3
47. Dan. 3:13–26
48. Lev. 21
49. Rev. 12:6
50. Rev. 20:1–2
51. Gen. 11:4-5

"Jesus" Looking Down on Man

Song

Some of us goes from days to weeks and years
Thinking that we know what sacrifices are.
But I'm here to tell you all
That Jesus paid and gave the greatest sacrifice.
Yes, he did! (repeat)
While Jesus was on the cross
What did he see?
He saw love and hate battling at his feet.
For those who choose "Love," then heaven awaits them.
For those who choose "Hate," then damnation awaits them.
My Lord
I'm struggling down here beneath your feet
Trying to make sense of it all.
The road map that you left which is our Bible
Teaches us that love and hate will always exist
Until you, my Lord, returns to make things right again.
For now, I'm choosing love
Love for my fellow man
Love for my Lord and Savior.
Yes, Lord, I'm choosing eternal life and not death.
Now is the time for everyone to choose
Is it life or death?

I hear the word *life*
But are you living the words of Jesus?
If not, then you have chosen damnation to your soul,
It's not too late my brethren
Make a change now and heaven will be waiting on you.

Heaven or hell is what it all boils down too.
Everything else is short lived and will come to an end.
I am choosing life, my Lord.

My brethren
The life you live is from the choices that you have made.
Take ownership of your life
Never blame or use excuses as a crutch.
Remember, Jesus is looking down … on us all
And his love remains the greatest sacrifice … for us all.

Second Song
Prayer

Lord Jesus
Every road that I have taken
Lead me back to you, my Lord.
No longer will I look at my feet.
I will lift my head as seeing you, "Jesus"
As if you were staring down…down on me.
It is my understanding that the road signs in life
All boils back to your crucifixion.
To accept Jesus as your Lord and Savior
Means to me that you have chosen life.
This is why I look to Jesus everybody.
Yes, Lord, I look to you; I look to you.
When all my hopes and strength are gone
Through you, I can be strong.
I look to you.
Everybody, who do you look too?
Please don't tell me

Look up and tell Jesus.
Like seeing him on the cross.
Yes, Lord, I look to you
I look to you.
When all my strength is gone
Through you, I can be strong.
I look to you.
Pause!
Only through Jesus can we see...the Father.
In his Father's house, there are many, many mansions.
There is room for us all that have chosen to believe.
Jesus looking down on man.
The right hand of God is our Lord and Savior "Jesus."
And Jesus will always be looking down, down on me.
Amen!

Comments

The song title left two songs in my heart. The second song is a prayer being sang, but after Pause is testimony. As I reflect back in my mind, there was no one saying take me as a sacrifice. Since no one was worthy, our God loved us so much and sent his son "Jesus." Nothing more to add, I was convinced that there was a God, and by his love for mankind, his Son paid the price for the world. The world witnessed Jesus dying and was the congregation for the *sacrifice*.

Ten Miles

Song

One day while driving on the interstate
I was ten miles out from my home
And I didn't remember those last ten miles.
So I did asked myself, who was at the wheel?
(ch) It had to be Jesus!
Listen, no one was in the car with me.
(ch) It had to be, oh yes, had to be our Lord and Saviour.
Jesus was my co-pilot and He took the wheel.
Yes He did, steered me from harm
Brought me from a might a long way.
(ch) It had to be, just had to be our Saviour!
I am seeing you as you are seeing me.
*I'm alive today as a testimonial that myself is living proof.
Jesus is alive and well.
If I didn't stay prayed up
Just where would I have been
If not for Jesus.
(ch) I'll tell you, it had to be Jesus.
I'm telling you that it was
That it was our Lord Jesus.
Let me say it again
While driving down the road

I felled asleep or felled short
Jesus took the wheel.
He brought me all the way home.
*(ch) It had to be the Lord!
Ladies and gentlemen
Put Jesus in your lives
When you fall short, Jesus will bring you home.
(ch) Jesus did brought you home.
Yes He did! (repeat)
Being a Saviour means you are saved countless time.
It had to be
It had to be
The only one worthy enough to die for all our sins
And to save me at the wheel.

Comment:

For extended version the asterisk are there from beginning to the
end. The choir will end this song for the extended version.

Spiritually Clean House

Song

Every day, I find myself cleaning my home, and no matter what
I do, dust is still there, somewhere.

Now, I must clean my spirit, but I need help from the Lord.

The dust in my spirit is my impurities and iniquities.

Furniture polish does clean dust in a house.

Only God, and, but God, cleans impurities and iniquities in
your spirit.

This formula is patented since the beginning from the garden
of Eden.

Just try it!

My neighbor once told me that there are no spiderwebs in
her house.

I had to show her that she was wrong.

To her surprise, she didn't see them.

It's the same for your spiritual cleansing.

Only God, and, but God, sees and cleans impurities and iniquities.

You just need to pray for the formula, and he will deliver.

Are there any spider webs in your house?

If your answer is no, it's because you are blinded by their existence.

Ask God to remove the spider webs in your home and in
your spirit.

The power is in his hands.

If your house is clean and there are still spiders in your home.
The spiders that remain are not harmful and are placed there as
     protection against other pests.
Only God, and, but God, can shield and protect you in your home.
This formula was patented since the garden of Eden.
If it was good back, then it's great right now.
Why don't you ... just try him?

Thought I Was in Heaven

Song

Listen to this, everybody!
I had a dream last night.
From that dream, I died and went to heaven.
JC was there, giving out chores in heaven.
I started to complain after receiving the same chores
Over and over
And about the heat.
JC overheard my complaint
Called me into his office.
He said, "Son, what seems to be the problem?"
I told him the problem.
He rudely said, "Do you know where the hell you are at?"
I said, "Yes, I'm in heaven."
He laughed for a minute, then said, "This is hell!"
You can complain all that you want; it won't do you any good.
JC then said, "There are times when complaining does not get
    you nowhere."
This I'll say is one of those times.
As I was leaving his office, he noticed that I was calling him JC.
He politely said, "That is not my name."
My name is Satan or Lucifer.
I immediately woke up and found myself still in bed.

I am here to tell you all, stop complaining because hell won't stand for it either.

Besides that, there is no cold water down below.

To be sure, ask for cold water immediately.

If no cold water, then you are not in heaven.

Cold water and the fiery lakes of hell don't mix!

This was only a dream

But it felt so real.

Comments

Our Father does speak to us through dreams. We just have to listen and find ways to give/take constructive criticism with our fellow man here on earth; if you cannot promote improvement or development, then why complain.

JC stands for Jesus Christ.

Filthy Rags

Oh, holy heavenly Father, I stand before you as a filthy rag.

I don't have much, but what I do have is all yours.

While your Son was on the cross, he was bruised, scorned, clothes was torn, and all that I could feel was the goodness in his heart for me.

So this day, I'm praising you from within.

Oh, Lord, please forgive me for my sins.

Among the people, I am nobody because I am judge with what I have on.

But you, Lord, you forgave me for my sins.

Still, am I dress for your kingdom?

While up on the cross, you gave up your image and paid through your sacrifice to keep our souls from being lost.

Through you, my Lord, my filthy rags are replaced with your Holy Spirit of embrace.

And I want to say, "Thank you for giving your all for me."

I can only imagine with reasoning that clothes cover the body of one and not the heart within me.

I'm at your mercy, my Lord, and I want to say, "Thank you," from me.

Amen!

Bedtime Song 2

Song/Prayer/Poem

Our Father
Before I slumber to sleep
I pray through Jesus
For my soul to keep.
In a brief moment
I am reflecting in my mind to what a day
That I had.
Never to take granted for being happy or sad.
Jesus, hear my prayer.
Through you, O Lord, I am at peace and never in despair.
In the morning just before I rise
I give you, Lord, my gratitude for waking me below the skies
While I was asleep, my divine safety was in your hands
That was made possible through an angel in this land.
Each day, my eyesight gets weaker
And my steps get a little slower.
Lord, I thank you anyway for the sight that I do have
And the steps that I do possess.
There are sometimes that I'll forget to praise your name.
To only be reminded of your pain and suffering
That you shed on the cross.

O, my God, this prayer that I'm sending up is not asking
for anything.

It's a prayer giving you all the glory for keeping my soul from
being lost.

This prayer is a prayer of praises and honoring your name.

Sweet dreams await me!

And the thoughts of continuing to glorify your name.

Amen, my heavenly Father!

Amen again through my Jesus's holy name!

I Believe in Miracles

Song/Testimonial

Sometime ago, I was searching for something, and not knowing, it was a prayer away.

You may ask, what could it have been what I was searching for?

I am not ashamed to say, it was Jesus.

I've made the discovery that worldly love doesn't last forever. But the love by our God is for eternity.

Once the search was over, miracles began to happen with no explanations in sight.

You must admit, that love is bigger than life itself.

With all the great things in life, we as his followers need to share them.

I want to share Jesus with you.

But, first, you must accept him in your heart as your Lord and Savior.

Then, and only then, you are on the path to a miracle in the making.

Be aware of your friends around you that may not know you anymore.

(Ch) That's all right!

Just remember, your friends don't have heaven or hell to put you in.

Make a connection to Jesus before it's too late.

Miracles do happen for a reason; it reminds us where the true power does lay.

The true power lies with Jesus.

This power was given to him by God Almighty.

As I remembered from reading the Bible, all authority in heaven and on earth has been given to Jesus.

I believe Jesus is the answer to our hopes and prayers. Miracles start and end with Jesus.

(Ch) We believe in Je … sus.

(Ch) We believe in mir … a … cles.

(Ch) We believe Jesus's love will last to eter … ni … ty.

There would be no one greater than he.

(Ch) Our Lord does believe in you and me.

Oh, yes, that's what a miracle means to me.

You see, I was lost; now I can see; Jesus is the miracle in me.

Oh, yes, Jesus is the miracle for us all that has chosen him as our Lord and Savior.

By giving testimony to God's power, Jesus is the miracle for all hearts that had chosen him to be.

I believe Jesus is our miracle because he died for you and me.

GPS to Heaven

God's Place Side Exit

Song

> From a dream that I had
> While riding on the freeway one morning.
> I decided to take the route to heaven.
> So I programmed my GPS, and it gave me no exits.
> I knew right away that I was using the wrong thing.
> If you are using GPS made by man, you won't see the exits
> to heaven.
> You must use the GPS made by God to find your way.
> So I began to call on the Holy Ghost to connect me to
> God's GPS.
> Then suddenly!
> All routes began to show up!
> Now, GPS means "God's Place Side Exit."
> I couldn't help but notice, it also gave the route to hell.
> So I'm asking everyone to pay close attention to your GPS.
> The wrong turn may take you down below.
> Steady your eyes on the prize and don't be distracted by
> any means.
> My next stop is heaven, and I can see the exit up ahead.
> Lord Jesus, I am on my way to heaven.

It won't be long, my GPS is showing the next exit.
I'm slowing down, making sure not to miss my exit.
Lord, Lord, Lord!
It is good to be on the right exit to heaven.
I can see the gates saying, "God's house, proceed with faith." All
    I could say was,
"Thank you, Lord. I made it.
Oh, thank you, Lord, I made it in your kingdom.
Yes, yes, yes! I made it."

Comments

When a person is sick for a long time, vision of their death may come in a dream. From being obedient to God, a glimpse of you landing faithfully in heaven may come.

Biblical Truth and Answers

Part 2

Frequently Asked Biblical Questions

1. In Genesis, a river watering the garden flowed from ___ ; from there, it was separated into ____ headwaters.

    Answer: a. Asshur, three b. Eden, two c. Eden, four

2. In Genesis, which river winds through the entire land of Havilah, where there is gold?

    A: a. Pishon b. Gihon c. Tigris d. Euphrates

3. Q: In "The Tower of Babel," the city was called ____ ?

    A: a. Canaan b. Shinar c. Gerar

4. Q: What book is after 2 Chronicles in the Bible?

    A: a. Judges b. Nehemiah c. Ezra d. Job

5. Q: How many divisions is the book of Psalms?

    A: a. Four b. Five c. Six d. Three

6. Q: How old was Noah when the floodwaters came upon the earth?

    A: a. Four hundred b. Five hundred c. Six hundred

7. Q: In Noah's time, how many days did the floodwaters continue to come upon the earth?

    A: a. Thirty b. Forty c. Fifty

8. Q: How old was Noah when he died?

    A: a. 750 b. 850 c. 950

9. When Abram was ninety-nine years old, the Lord appeared to him and said, "I Am who I Am; walk before me and be blameless."

   A: True or False

10. Q: Altogether, Abraham lived a hundred and seventy-five years. Then Abraham breathed his last and died. His sons Isaac and Ishmael buried him with which one of his wives?

    A: a. Sarah b. Hagar c. Keturah

11. Q: Besides the book of Esther, what other female name is a book in the Bible?

    A: a. Naomi b. Ruth c. Hannah

12. Although Jesus is not the physical son of Joseph, he is the legal son and therefore a descendant of David.

    A: True or False

13. The _____ were a legalistic and separatistic group who strictly, but often hypocritically, kept the laws of Moses and the unwritten "tradition of the elders."

    A: a. Pharisees b. Sadducees c. Nazarene

14. The _____ were more worldly and politically minded and were theologycally unorthodox, among other things, denying the resurrection, angels, and spirits.

    A: a. Pharisees b. Sadducees c. Nazarene

The following answers and questions were taken out of the *Holman QuickSource Bible Dictionary.*

15. Jesus's proper name derives from the Hebrew Joshua, meaning "Yahweh saves" or "salvation is from Yahweh" (Matt. 1:21). *Christ* is the Greek term for "," equivalent to the Hebrew *Messiah*.

    A: a. Anointed b. Savior c. Redeemer

16. Q: He was an outstanding missionary, theologian, and writer of the early church, who was this person?

    A: a. Saul b. Paul c. Barnabas

17. Q: Under the Old Testament, the Ten Commandments were referred as the ?

   A: a. Bill of Rights b. God's words c. Decalogue

18. Q: Who was the high priest at the time of the trial and crucifixion of Jesus?

   A: a. Caiaphas b. Melchizedek c. Amos

19. Q: Which origin is *YHWH?*

   A: a. Greek b. Hebrew c. Aramaic

20. Hallelujah is an exclamation of praise that recurs frequently in the book of Psalms meaning "praise Yahweh!"

   A: a. True or False

The following questions and answers were taken out of the Zondervan NIV Study Bible.

21. Q: In the genealogy of Jesus, how many generations in all from Abraham to David?

   A: a. 12 b. 14 c. 16

22. Q: In the genealogy of Jesus, how many generations in all from David to the exile to Babylon?

   A: a. 10 b. 14 c. 16

23. Q: In the genealogy of Jesus, how many generations in all from the exile to Christ?

   A: a. 12 b. 14 c. 16

24. Q: After John the Baptist's disciples came and took his body and buried it, whom did they tell?

   A: a. Jesus b. His wife c. His mother

25. Q: According to the Bible, who did Jesus appear to last after his death?

   A: a. Peter b. James c. Paul

26. Q: King Darius made a decree that during the next thirty days, anyone who prays to any god or man except to him

would be thrown into the lion's den. Who disobeyed his decree?

A: a. Daniel b. James c. Peter

27. God ordered to marry an adulterous wife, Gomer, and their three children were each given a symbolic name representing part of the ominous message.

A: a. Micah b. Hosea c. Amos

28. Q: Which book of the Bible is the shortest?

A: a. Obadiah b. Jude c. Philemon

29. Q: *Jehovah's Witness* was recognized by the *Webster's* Dictionary in what year?

A: a. 1910 b. 1925 c. 1932

30. Q: *Jehovah* is a word in the dictionary derived from *Yehowah* of the Hebrew word Yahweh, which came from YHWH. What year did the Webster's Dictionary establish a date?

A: a. 1530 b. 1640 c. 1700

31. Q: *Christian* is a word the Webster's Dictionary recognized in what year?

A: a. 1500 b. 1526 c. 1560

32. Q: What year did *Webster's Dictionary* give for *Presbyterian?*

A: a. 1600 b. 1641 c. 1741

33. Q: What year did the *Webster's Dictionary* give for *Methodist?*

A: a. 1593 b. 1693 c. 1700

34. Q: What year did the *Webster's Dictionary* give for Protestant?

A: a. 1539 b. 1649 c. 1705

35. Q: In the book of Jeremiah, who was the false prophets?

A: a. Hananiah b. Shemaiah c. Zedekiah

36. The three major prophets (Isaiah, Jeremiah, Ezekiel) and Zephaniah all have the same basic sequence of messages:

(1) oracles against Israel, (2) oracles against the nations, (3) consolation for Israel; is this statement true or false?

A: a. True b. False

37. Q: In 1 Kings, King Solomon had how many wives?

A: a. 450 b. 600 c. 700

38. In addition to King Solomon's wives, he had how many concubines?

A: a. 100 b. 200 c. 300

39. In 6/5 BC, Christ was born.

A: a. True b. False

40. In AD 7/8, Christ stood in the temple at the age of eleven.

A: a. True b. False

41. In AD 27/28, John the Baptist was imprisoned.

A: a. True b. False

42. In AD 29/30, John the Baptist died.

A: a. True b. False

43. Q: Which book of the Bible did God reveal first his true name?

A: a. Genesis b. Exodus c. Number

44. Symbolically, the number seven stands for ...

A: a. Unity b. Nothing at all c. Completeness

45. Q: What is a part of man's body that has been the blame for so many wars?

A: a. Hand b. Feet c. Tongue

Next questions and answers will be coming out of *Holman QuickSource Bible Dictionary*.

46. Q: What does *Jehovah-Jireh* mean?

A: a. Yahweh is peace b. Yahweh will provide c. Yahweh is my banner

47. Q: What does *Jehovah-Nissi* mean?

A: a. Yahweh is peace   b. Yahweh will provide   c. Yahweh is my banner

48. Q: What does *Jehovah-Shalom* mean?

A: a. Yahweh is peace   b. Yahweh will provide   c. Yahweh is my banner

49. Q: What does *Jehovah-Shamma* mean?

A: a. Yahweh is peace   b. Yahweh will provide   c. The Lord is there

50. Q: What does *Jehovah-Tsidkenu* mean?

A: a. The Lord is our righteousness   b. The Lord is there   c. The Lord is the Lord

51. Q: What does the word *Torah* mean?

A: a. Law   b. Sin   c. Place of birth

52. Q: What does the name *Moses* mean?

A: a. Drawn out of the water   b. Baby in the basket   c. Piece of cloth

53. *YHWH* is known by the technical term tetragrammaton (Gk., meaning "four letters"). The written Hebrew language did not include vowels.

A: a. True   b. False

54. Q: The word *amen* means what?

A: a. so be it   b. to affirm the truth   c. truthful and faithful   d. all the above

At this time, questions and answers must come to an end. I've enjoyed the time it took to write and to share precious time it would take to answer these questions. My name is Gregory Dixon, and remember, everyone is welcome in God's house! By now, we should have a good understanding that our God does not favor points in this test, but putting your faith into your work, he finds great favor within. Each question is worth two points. Top score is 108.

Biblical Truth and Answers

Part 2

Answer Sheet

1. _____
2. _____
3. _____
4. _____
5. _____
6. _____
7. _____
8. _____
9. _____
10. _____
11. _____
12. _____
13. _____
14. _____
15. _____
16. _____
17. _____
18. _____

19. _____

20. _____

21. _____

22. _____

23. _____

24. _____

25. _____

26. _____

27. _____

28. _____

29. _____

30. _____

31. _____

32. _____

33. _____

34. _____

35. _____

36. _____

37. _____

38. _____

39. _____

40. _____

41. _____

42. _____

43. _____

44. _____

45. _____

46. _____

47. _____

48. _____

49. _____

50. _____

51. _____

52. _____

53. _____

54. _____

Biblical Truth and Answers

Part 2

Answers

Each question is worth two points. Top score is 108.

1. c
2. a
3. b
4. c
5. b
6. c
7. b
8. c
9. False
10. A
11. b
12. True
13. a
14. b
15. a
16. b
17. c

18. a

19. b

20. True

21. b

22. b

23. b

24. a

25. c

26. a

27. b

28. c

29. c

30. a

31. b

32. b

33. a

34. a

35. a, b

36. a

37. c

38. c

39. a

40. b

41. a

42. b

43. b

44. c

45. c

46. b

47. c

48. a

49. c

50. a

51. a

52. a

53. a

54. d

Biblical Truth and Answers

Part 2

References

1. Gen. 2:10
2. Gen. 2:11
3. Gen. 11:1–2.
4. Table of contents
5. Introduction: Psalm
6. Gen. 7:6
7. Gen. 7:17
8. Gen. 9:28–29
9. Gen. 17:1
10. Gen. 25:7–10
11. Ruth Introduction (Title)
12. Matt. 1:16
13. Matt. 3:7 (notes)
14. Matt. 3:7 (notes)
15. Page 190 (Jesus Christ)
16. Page 273 (Paul)
17. Page 348 (Ten Commandments)
18. Page 55 (Caiaphas)

19. Page 220 (Lord)

20. Page 144 (Hallelujah)

21. Matt. 1:17

22. Matt. 1:17

23. Matt. 1:17

24. Matt. 14:12

25. Luke 24:6 (Resurrection Appearances)

26. Dan. 6:10–14

27. Hos. 1

28. Philem.

29. Dictionary

30. Dictionary

31. Dictionary

32. Dictionary

33. Dictionary

34. Dictionary

35. Jer. 28 and 29

36. Intro Ezekiel Literary Features

37. 1 Kings 11:3

38. 1 Kings 11:3

39. New Testament Chronology

40. Same

41. Same

42. Same

43. Exod. 3:14

44. Intro: Revelation Distinctive Feature

45. Jas. 3:5–7

46. Page 186

Adam and Eve (Genesis)

Testimonial

In the garden of Eden, God created man in his image and named him Adam. His only job was to worship God. By the power of the Lord, Adam was given dominion (rule) over the earth in body and in mind (the total package). But Adam was saddened due to everything on earth had a mate except him. Note: The previous statement is a mind concept in connection to his rule or dominion. God could tell that he was unhappy and put Adam in a deep sleep. From his womb and in the evening, a rib was removed, and God made woman. Note: The previous statement is a concept concerning the body in connection to his rule or dominion. Her name would be Eve. Adam and Eve were joined together by God. Adam and Eve was the first marriage. But Eve was new to the world, and it was Adam's responsibility to teach her the way that God intended for them to live in the garden.

While in heaven, God created his first angel named Satan/Lucifer. Satan was jealous of Adam being favored by God. Satan entered the garden as a serpent and told Eve if she eats from the tree of the knowledge of good and evil, she will be like God. So Eve ate from the tree and gave Adam (her husband) some of the fruit as well. Both of them saw for the first time that they were naked. God being the Father knew his children had committed a bad act. Both of them were cast out of the garden for disobeying God. Satan(s) was cursed and cast out of heaven for his part and now stands as an adversary against God. In my mind, Adam's decision to eat the fruit was decided by Eve. Eve was not totally faultless because Adam was given dominion over everything before God made Eve. Adam was just as guilty because his helpmate and he are one. A rib from Adam made Eve, flesh of his flesh, bone of his bone, and was the first marriage. From my last statement, a rib from Adam extended dominion to Eve for the species of mankind. Men are placed at the head of a family for being made first, and this is the natural order according to the Bible.

In the KJV, the word *helpmeet* is a term for woman as a helper precisely adapted to man (Genesis 2:18). Modern translations supply various equivalents: help suitable for him (NASB, NIV); help as his partner (NRSV); a suitable companion for him (TEV). The noun translated "help" or "partner" does not suggest subordination. The adjective meet (translated "suitable," "comparable," or "corresponding") stresses that woman, unlike the animals (Genesis 2:20), can be truly one with man (2:24), that is, enjoy full fellowship and partnership in humanity's God-given task (Genesis 1:27–28) of rule and dominion. Women in the Eastern Nations still carry on like in the old days, but Western women are sometimes eager to be the head and play a leadership role in our churches. My point is simple: Adam knew the old way kept them in the garden of Eden. Eve, on the other hand, did know but was easily persuaded by Satan. Our Bible is an account of things in the past and things to come in the future; please do not stray too far and lose favor with God. If a female has been anointed to act in a leadership role in the church, then she should as God commanded her to do so. The Bible does not take into account of Western civilization and does not show many women in leadership roles in our past churches; when women call on the name of Jesus, they will rise like Jesus did from the grave. We all have access to his name, and many of us do not understand that his name is power and is all we need in this life and for eternal life. If you still remain focused on the Bible to indicate women not mentioned in the Bible for not having leadership roles in the church, you are focused on no basis clearly not saying women can or cannot. Jesus should be your only focus.

Therefore, I wish you well, my sisters, follow Jesus as commanded; we as people do not have heaven or hell to put anyone in.

This testimonial was put in my spirit by my deacon (Jimmy Butler) and another deacon (Darryl Edwards) on a Sunday morning before church service; we have children who are eager to serve God. Let's not stand in their way. Jesus was twelve years old and was committed to his Father's business. His business is to save souls. Genesis is one of the five books that Moses wrote and gives a complete account of the beginning. Among the farmers, there is an old saying, "If good seeds are planted, then good crops are yield." Within our youth, we must plant good seeds, then and only then we will see the fruits of our labor. Good seeds are morals, respect, and love for our fellow man. Before any crops are planted, there is always a beginning. The garden of Eden was the beginning and awaits everyone chosen to enter the kingdom of God.

Adam and Eve 2

Two lead singers (Lead 1 is Adam, and Lead 2 is Eve)

Song

(Lead 1) While we were in the garden
Here comes Eve!
She is walking toward me with something in her hand.
Oh, Lord, what could it be?
What could it be in her hand?
So she handed me not only a fruit
But the forbidden fruit.
My Lord, what must I do?
So I took it and ate it
And we didn't die.
But we saw each other naked
And hid from our God that stays above the sky.
Oh, my Lord, what must we do?
So we covered our bodies
With fig leaves, never to see each other without shame
Eve and I.
God came down and knew that we had committed a bad sin.
(Lead 2) Lord, it was that serpent who told me. If we eat from
    that tree
We surely won't die, and we would be …like God,

Adam and I.
But he lied, and you all will see
And now me and Adam is casted out of our home
Where we are never to be!
(Lead 1) Yes, Lord! We didn't obey you.
Now, we are out of the garden
Never to reenter again, and now we must flee.
Everything was good when we obeyed our Lord.
Please, everyone, follow our Lord.
Satan has brought sin (death) upon us.
*After death, Adam and Eve reflected back in spirit only!
(Lead 2) But God had a plan
The plan was second Adam called Jesus.
Isn't that just like a *father*!
To give his right hand (Jesus)
When his children are in need.
(Leads 1 and 2) Here we are, Jesus,
(Lead 1) Eve and I.
We'll await your return
We will, we will await your return
While kneeling down … on … one knee.
(Lead 2) Oh, yes, we will! (Repeat)
Yes, Lord!
(Leads 1 and 2) Return us back home
(Lead 1) Back to the garden that lies beneath your sky
(Lead 2) Adam and I.
(Leads 1 and 2) Amen!

Comments

This song is a duet between man and woman. If this song is sung by a married couple, it will give it full meaning; in this song, it's suggested that Eve knew God's plans for Jesus. She didn't in life, but in death, her spirit and Adam had to become aware of the second Adam. The asterisk (*) part is not to be sung but gives an outlook on their future based upon speculation.

Figuratively Speaking

Figuratively speaking, here's a mystery down below that keeps popping in my mind. Here are some words with their meaning to assist you. "Shepherd is a pastor, and congregation is a flock." The flock is made up of sheep and goats.

Mystery!

In any congregation, while at church, if a snake was physically seen in church, who would run out? To me, any congregation is made up of three types of people. There is the sheep, the goat, and the goat/sheep into one. Let's examine the sheep first. A timid defense creature or a timid docile person. Second is the goat. A licentious man. Licentious means "marked by disregard for strict rules of correction." Third is goat/sheep. This is a person who dispenses both behaviors at different times. At this time, the percentage shows fifty-fifty but can reflect various percentages. For example, 60-40, 70-30, or 45-55.

Back to the question from above!

My answer would be that the sheep will run all the way out to safety. The goats/sheep will run halfway but will continue to look back. The goats will stay to fight the snake or remove it because an urgency to remove is present. The goats/sheep may accompany the goats in the removal of the snake; in any congregation to my understanding, there exist the needs for all three.

For one to have spiritual growth, the church, which is the pasture, must allow you to graze in greener pastures. This does not mean to leave the church but to be put somewhere else and still be under the same pastor. There are some times that your spirit dictates one to leave to answer to a higher calling; *Jesus is the pastor for all time*. Therefore, men/women as pastors/shepherds come and go to where Jesus needs them to be. It is the same for the congregation as well. Pastoring/preaching is to be directed to the heart and soul of our fellow men first. In the first paragraph under *mystery*, a serpent was also seen in the garden of Eden. Confusion, panic, and fear were caused by the serpent. Adam and Eve were cast from the garden (greener pasture). Spiritually, our Bible teaches us how to battle the serpent; in any case, the serpent must be removed physically and spiritually for order to exist.

Eve was confused when the serpent told her that if she eats from the tree, she will be like God. Adam saw that Eve did not die after she had eaten from the tree. Adam and Eve were cast out of the garden, and their dominion was lost over the earth. Let's look at the three words: *confusion, panic, and fear*; with confusion and loss of dominion, panic and fear were born. My last statement is why animals fear us and why we fear the animals. There are some people in this world that would kill a complete harmless snake just for being a snake. As part of the grand design, snakes are responsible for keeping down the pest population. Rodents and pests are greatly responsible for crops being destroyed. Therefore, we must learn how to coexist together as our God intended; would your answer be the same as mine? This mystery is really serious, and I hope my point was received with an open mind. May the Lord continue to bless you, my brethren!

Doors of the Church Are Open

Song/Testimonial

After each sermon, my pastor will say, "The doors of this church are open."

During this time, a person who is looking for a church home or does not know the Lord can come to the front.

This is truly a happy occasion because we have another brother or sister to battle sin.

The first step that you make is not easy.

The second step is easy or harder depending on your faith and relationship with God.

As a member, I welcome you to our church family.

(Ch) So I want you come on down

If you don't have a church family, brethren, I beg you to come on down and take a seat.

With so much sin in the world, church is a good place to strengthen yourself in the fight against sin.

Time is or could be running out for me and you.

(Ch) Don't sit there any longer!

Ohoooooo! Jesus was the sacrificial Lamb that paid the price for our sins.

(Ch) It's time … to get on board!

Don't wait another minute!

(Ch) It's time … to get on board!

If not today, then when?
Brethren, it's time, time to get on board.
(Ch) It's time ... to get on board!
Make this day your day for the Lord.
There is strength in numbers!
As a flock of sheep and goats, wolves will try to get you alone.
  Sadly, you will fall victim to the dangers of this world.
(Ch) It's time ... to get on board! (Repeat)
Ohooooooo!
It's time!

Comment

Ohooooooo is a seasoning that I gave for this song; when you sing it, please use your own seasoning to make this song your song.

Author's Personal Comments
Hometown: Quincy, Florida

Second Elizabeth Missionary Baptist Church is my family church; in the cemetery, my father's family is on the left and on the right is my mother's family. My mother is buried alongside my father in his family plot. My grandfather, deceased deacon Empire Murray Sr., and my aunt Sarah Ann Dixon-Kirkland, sacrificed a lot of their time to the church. *Two* other persons that come to mind are deceased Frankie Taylor and deceased deacon Charlie Kendrick. They were not kin through blood, but through their strong and gentle spirit to everyone. I have to believe that their hearts were for the church. This is the only sense that I can begin to make out of it. To continue their legacy, the ministry must go forward further than the community. This is a new season and is time for a change. I am fifty-seven years old, and my age is 5.7 seconds compared to our Lord. Our maximum time here on earth is 120 years, which is twelve seconds. In Deuteronomy 31:1–8 and 34:7 is how I arrived with the maximum time here on earth.

A task has been handed down to me by my God, and I must carry it out in order to see his kingdom. Therefore, I don't have much time to waste. There is nothing on this earth more important than God's kingdom. Anything else is short-lived and will come to an end. Songs, poems, and testimonials will one day come to an end for me. But, for now, I have written more than 130 songs; with the combination of work and faith, I'll one day earn the prize. The prize is decided by my sweet Lord and

Savior

"Jesus"

having the

final

Word!

There are times that we must reach out further and stand on God's words. This is where our faith comes in. So many has been before me, but their experiences may have not gotten shared with the world. The federal government is the largest workforce in the United States. People with different ethnic backgrounds joined with strong ethics to make this country truly blessed. Our strength as a nation is based on this concept.

I will like to take this time to mention some of my greatest accomplishments in my twenty-six years working for the federal government. First: Joined the US Navy in 1979; after basic training, became an aviation structural mechanic, worked intermediate (AIMD) and organization (VF-114) level of maintenance. Survived close encounters of death while working on a flight deck of an aircraft carrier named the USS *Enterprise*. At that time, it was a West Coast ship.

Second: To leave the West Coast, I agreed to extend for orders to head back to the east. As a trained naval correctional counselor under special programs, I overturned a male sailor (Gallego) Bad Discharge at a brig in Philadelphia, Pennsylvania. The brig housed both men/women from all military branches of services. This young man was truly a testament to what our God can do through people. As a correctional counselor, it was my job to recognize service men/women salvageable to retain in the military. After Gallego was released from the brig, probation period was one year, I kept in touch with his progress until my end of service date; when the brig commanding officer relieved of command ceremony was held, he showed up returning the support that was rendered to him.

Third: In Tallahassee, Florida, I fell short and survived another close encounter with death while being arrested at a federal prison; it would seem that my God has a task for me, so maybe death is postponed in order to write religious songs, poems, and testimonials. Only my God knows! Fourth: Being married to Wanda after my end of duty in the military and for twenty-seven years. From our union is one son, but I have another son from my early military life.

My oldest son (Gabriel) is doing good, and he lives in Tennessee. Gabriel's mom and I both served in the Navy; we are the same age. She is my friend for life. Together, Wanda and I had a boy and a girl within our household. My stepdaughter (Sharonda) came out of high school and college all right. She graduated from high school in the top ten. I advised her to join the Reserve and have the military pay for her college; under the selective service program, you have to sign up once you are eighteen years of age. It's the law until you are above their age limit; why not join the Reserves and let the military pay for college? Any recruiter can explain providing that you can meet the criteria. Early good choices make less bumps in the road to success.

Sharonda has a family of her own now. When she broke her leg, I carried her from the car to the entrance of the hospital to have a cast made. Her mom and she laughed at me, and I still don't see the humor to this very day. I couldn't bear that she was in tears and pain. But I love them all to death because we keep on living through our kids. Having their best interest makes them our kids regardless being biological or not.

Those accomplishments are just a few but are essential for the making of the man that I became. My wife and I are not perfect, but we strive to be in God's kingdom. Perfect means that you don't need saving and you are above Satan's approach. "Satan has you, and you are not aware of it" was stated under "who is Satan." From the first to the fourth, Jesus was present then, and his presence is very strong now. I often wonder, when will God release me from my task? My answer is that God will never release me and will keep me closer to his bosom. The choice is mine to walk away. Walking away is not an option for me. With my last breath, I will be uttering the name Jesus. I believe that name is the master key to eternal life.

Let's continue to fight against sin a little further than our community. We can all make a difference if our God is first and we support one another in time of need. Come to Jesus, just now!

Conclusion

We have both; this is what makes a congregation. Figuratively speaking, sheep and goats are the physical makeup of my church. Our pastor (shepherd) has his hands full; if church was for the righteous, only a few would remain. To our readers, walk by faith and not by sight, and you'll be all right. Your faith cannot sit on the shelf; faith must be put to work.

Let us keep our focus on Jesus. If someone wants to give God a name, that's all right. True believers know where their help comes from. After reading this book, readers should know what God means to me, how to better understand what it means to try Jesus by putting him on trial, and one hundred questions that a Christian should know. In closing, stay in the Word of God and rely on the Holy Spirit for interpretation. Do something nice toward a complete stranger. It doesn't have to be money; it can be a prayer or buying them lunch. Any good thought or gesture toward he or she will show favor in the eyes of God. There is no doubt in my mind that one good deed toward mankind is the step to making this world a better place.

Special Addition

Correction Officer

Name: Gregory Dixon, Formal Federal Correctional Ofc.

Location: Tallahassee, Florida

Facilities: Federal Correctional institute (Female Prison)

Federal Detention Center (Men Jail)

Subject: Reliving the 2006 Sex Scandal in Tallahassee

Season: Summer

One morning, after sixteen hours working a double shift at the Female Federal Prison in Tallahassee, Florida, there was a commotion in the air that something just happened at the federal jail below. While in G-Unit, I could look down on the jail, but was unable to tell what was happening. My relief officer properly relieved me, and I was headed out. While exiting, I could see that the control room officer was busy; and I was waiting to see if I was needed by calling the lieutenant office. No answer, so I continued out toward the front entrance, then stopped and talked to the perimeter patrol officer. I am just glad that I didn't get in and ride around. I asked him if he knew what had happened, and he replied, "Shots were fired, and someone was hurt." I asked him if he knew who it was. He said, "An agent and a correctional officer were involved in a shooting."

While I was walking toward my vehicle, I could see a Caucasian female not being staff out the corner of my eye. Since she was outside and not in the prison, I thought nothing of it. I proceeded to my vehicle, and guns were drawn. A man's voice yelled out, "Get your hands up," and I was arrested. A male officer asked me, "Do you have any weapons?" and I responded by saying, "No." No explanation was given! The female from my peripheral vision was part of the arresting team. My vehicle was searched for weapons, but none was found. At this time, I didn't understand the urgency in the manner that the arrest transpired. I could have easily gotten killed after what transpired at the jail. It was that time and my last when I decided that working for my Lord was now my priority; "Why not work for God?" was my motivation to write religious songs and poems in hopes of earning my place in heaven. Simultaneously, there were other officers being arrested. I was detained with the other officers at the federal courthouse. While awaiting to go before the magistrate, apparently an indictment was issued on six officers. But one was killed in the shooting at the jail. A lawyer was assigned to me, and the magistrate viewed us as a menace to society.

We were represented by our own lawyers. We were sent separately to local nearby jails. Before going to Leon County Jail, I was interviewed by two agents. I informed them that no rights were read to me. So one of them read me my rights, and I declined talking to them. I spent one day in Leon County Jail wearing paper like clothing in a suicidal room and with an officer outside. Apparently, a female medical staff on duty observed my blood pressure being high and deemed me as suicidal to be safe. Twenty-three hours had passed, and I was exhausted.

The following day, I was sent to the jail in Thomasville, Georgia. The food was great, and the staff was doing their job. A female sergeant saw to my needs and was very professional under the existing conditions. I was visited by my captain, and he told me what had happened at the jail. My captain was a good captain that put first his people that are under him. My captain indicated that a lieutenant was injured also. That lieutenant injured was well-liked among the staff; *well-liked* means no "favoritism and respect is received." The lawyer assigned to me also visited me and said,

"There's no reason for you to be locked up pending trial." A week and a half had passed, and I was transported back to Tallahassee to go before the federal judge. After listening to both sides, he decided to release us under supervision.

My wife was waiting out back to pick me up, because the news media were waiting also. We ran into the press, but as standard procedure, the judge said not to talk about this case; we finally left the courthouse and returned home. Under the supervision, I was fitted with a leg monitor, assigned a probation officer to visit me, and to call if the need arose for me to go somewhere. While awaiting to go to trial, I was informed by my lawyer that one of the codefendants suffered a stroke. Two other codefendants pleaded out; it only left myself and another officer to be tried together.

My lawyer reminded me of the plea deal, but I told him specifically what I was guilty of and to tell the court on my behalf. I heard testimony from inmates, who I knew, were lying. Their testimonies didn't matter, but their agreement to lie was to benefit themselves. To me, they were compensated to lie. What was it being offered, I don't know, maybe sentence reductions? Testimonies were given by inmates saying that they were the lookout for me. This never happened because the sex acts were done at night and with one person working on the compound. After count, there was a large time lapse, just after the 10:00 p.m. (2200) and after the 12:01 a.m. (0001) count. My lawyer was informed by me that there was possibly an investigation at the prison that never made it to trial. You see, three inmates were placed in the special housing unit for having sex and smoking drugs with me. They were tested on multiple occasions, and their urinalysis results were negative, while in G-Unit, an inmate just released from SHU heard my name and said, "You are the reason that I was placed in SHU." She didn't know me, but she claimed that the inmate community told the SIA this.

Their names are Ashley Cartrette, Crystal Compton, and Tameka Brown. According to this inmate, they were questioned repeatedly, tested for drugs again and again, and they still stayed committed to the truth. My reasoning for mentioning their names is to bring attention to their unfair treatment and in hopes that someone will make this right. It was fitting to compensate inmates for lying. It should be equally fitting to compensate inmates for telling the truth. The SIA was a lieutenant that showed favoritism before being promoted to this position.

Some subordinates could call him by first name. Supervisors have rules and policies to govern subordinates. Once those rules are applied differently to some staff, that is the favoritism. Very possibly, another crime(s) was committed but never brought to the attention of the court; under the Brady rule, all prior investigation revolving around me being favorable or not should have been provided. The SIA is responsible for providing the prosecution with any prior investigations. The special investigative agent is assigned to the same facility and to that warden. The prosecution was asked twice, "Was there any other investigation?" and according to him, the SIA said, "No." Later, I will include two complaints indicating people placed in authoritative position can easily violate the law or someone's civil liberties and be held accountable for their actions. My lawyer and I decided to face my own alleged charges and for me to focus on their part later. My admission of guilt was to introducing contraband for sex like gum and cigarettes. There were four inmates whose charges were filed, but one was dropped due to that she wanted nothing in return. Those items mentioned can acquire stamps, which is like money within a prison. Also, an inmate can have money put into another inmate commissary's account by someone outside the prison. After all the evidence and testimonies were heard, the jury came back dismissing all the other charges that I had nothing to do with; chief justice announced the sentencing date.

Before the sentencing took place, my lawyer was informed by me that I wanted to start doing my time right away. Upon entering court, I was dressed for it. The sentence was one year in prison and three years under supervision. I asked my lawyer to ask the judge for one more day. A year and a day would subject me to good conduct time, meaning early release.

As I look back, I can remember the staff talking about perimeter patrol officers harassing a staff that lost his life. Perimeter patrol is an armed post that patrols the perimeter of the facility. The deceased officer was put at the jail due to new assignment. Anytime an officer is in trouble, they can be assigned to the jail to work. Staff know immediately that you are under investigation due to new assignment. Myself and the other staff indicted were never put on new assignment. My thoughts are that the deceased officer became a time bomb. Previous staff placed on new assignment that are non-correctional staff receive the same harassment. It was said that the deceased had AIDS—maybe not, I don't know. This talk could have easily been harassment. Staff made comments on his hair resembling the alien movie *Predator*. Only a few agents were sent to make the arrest and were not expecting gunfire. At any federal prison or jail, staff are not allowed to bring weapons on the ground of the facility. Any staff working could potentially have a weapon because no screening was required. For having a weapon such as a gun is more serious than the alleged charges. In a prison setting, you are under stress, with long hours, interacting with inmates to resolve problems or fights and ensuring the prison is free of weapons by searches. These are just a few of the many duties, and many staff members do their job very well.

Prior complaints at FCI Tallahassee:

1. The promotion board was unfair among the correctional staff. This problem was reported to the union president. Later, a mediator was summoned to the facility to hear the complaints of staff; it was revealed that prior practices indicated applications for promotion were not being looked at. By not looking at the applications, everyone made the best qualified list, which means the board could promote anyone they choose. The mediator declared that the promotion board was wrong by doing this. The mediator insisted on a cutoff to be established and to read each application based on merits, not favoritism.

2. Correctional staff on day shift were expected to be at work fifteen minutes early for briefing without being paid. This complaint was also corrected, and staff received settlement based on their years.

Reflection

These are not individual complaints and were dealt with using the bargain agreement process. No violence was used to resolve them. My reason for mentioning the above two complaints is to show people in authority can violate someone's civil liberties. After twenty-six years working for the federal government, I think I've worked for the very best. My tour of duty consisted of twelve years in the United States Navy and fourteen years for a federal prison system. This story is my testimonial! May God continue to keep me and to bless my trespassers. There are some times wherein if the evildoers think their deeds are in the dark, once exposed to the light, a change will come. I am no exception to my previous statement. The light is on someone else now to correct for not knowing the full truth. Once again, we as people find ourselves falling short, and we need Jesus to make things right through the righteous.

In the military, there is an old saying: "Pen is mightier than the sword." The pen indicates nonviolence and the opportunity to be heard while seeking resolution. By doing this, we tried to avoid a hostile work environment; if there are small wars within a house, then divided it will fall. From a military objective, the war (fight) is lost. Favoritism can divide a house, and in the military, it was not welcome; if any form of harassment is directed to anyone, I hope that co-workers reconsider before emotions spin out of control.

When Jesus comes, a new season he will bring. Once this change occurs, we won't be slaves to our petty differences anymore. I offer my condolences to both officers' families, who lost their loved ones. I give my God all the praises and the glory for the strength to write this book. Thank you, Lord!

Note

Under "Special Addition," these songs to follow and testimonials included are very important to me. I hope that they give you great comfort because they all are from my heart. Always remember, by knowing and believing, our God has the final word.

Pardon Me, Lord

Song

A while ago on a Sabbath day
I was running a little late wearing mismatched socks
And headed to a Sunday service.
*Look up!
Pardon me, my Lord!
There are some times that we forget how precious time is
Also, forgetting that we don't have control over time.
*Look straight into the audience!
But one thing that I can assure you all of
Is that you don't want heaven to close its doors or gates.
(Ch) Pardon me!
Pardon me, Lord, for not keeping better track of your time.
Pardon me, Lord, for driving too fast trying to save time.
Pardon me, Lord, for being the way that I am.
(Ch) Pardon me!
Pardon me, Lord, for not being quiet in church.
Pardon me, Lord, for using my cell phone in your sanctuary.
Pardon me, Lord, for being the way that I am.
Yes, my, Lord, the way that I am!
(Ch) Lord, will you pardon me?
Will *you* pardon me, Lord, for not being a cheerful giver?

Will you pardon me, Lord, for not having my own Bible in
   my hand?
Will you pardon me, Lord, for not extending a helping hand?
Yes, yes to my fellow man?
Pardon me, Lord, for being the way that I am.
Yes, Lord, the way that I am!
(Ch) Pardon me for the way that I am really, my Lord!
Pause!
If this song is offensive to someone
Then ... pardon me.
Pardon me, Lord, for not doing the best that I can.
Pardon me, Lord, for being the way that I am.
(Ch) Pardon me! (Repeat three times)
Jesus is the king that died for us all to be forgiven.
Jesus ... will forgive me for the way that I am.
(Ch) Pardon me, my Lord! (Repeat)
Pardon me, Lord, for being the way that ... I ... am.

Comments

The word *pardon* can be easily replaced with *forgive*. The asterisk
(*) is the indication for direction for the singer. By asking for
forgiveness, swipe your slate clean before God. There is a word for
this; it's called *repent*.

Lord, Slow Me Down

*Look up!
My Lord, I must apologize for my unfaithfulness.
Please, God, have mercy and forgive me for my past sins.
Help me, my Lord, to slow down and to focus on you.
Help me to stop running from you
But to start running toward my help in you, my Lord.
(Ch) Lord, help us all to stop running from you.
Please, my Lord, have mercy
Slow me down so that my focus is on you.
Help me to stop running from you.
(Ch) Lord, help us all
Yes, yes
To stop running from you.
Lord, put me on cruise control to your Holy Spirit.
Slow me down
Slow me down, Jesus.
Slow me down to a speed so that I can remain focused on you.
(Ch) Put us on cruise control to your Holy Spirit.
*Look into the audience.
Listen, everyone, when you break the speed limit
You may receive a ticket or crash leading up to
Injury or death, it is the same for the Lord.

Warnings, you will receive
Injuries, you will receive
Death, you may receive twice.
*Look up!
(Ch) Slow me down, Jesus.
Put me on a speed to your holy name.
Slow me down; slow me down, Jesus
Lord, I want to avoid the second death.
(Ch) Slow me down! (Repeat)
*Look into the audience.
Jesus can slow all of us down
To avoid hell (death)
And make us heaven-bound.
Paused! Look up!
(Ch) Slow me down, Jesus! (Repeat)
*Look into the audience.
To everyone, say, "Slow me down, Jesus!"

Comments

Cell phones and walking around with headphones listening to music is distracting us in our environment; we are out of control, meaning that we are going too fast to look around and give caution when needed. Slow down, and maybe another life would not have to suffer due to carelessness on our part. In the song above, you may get the idea that I am referring to driving, but I am not. It is referring to destination (heaven) and the reminder that warnings, injuries, and deaths will occur if we don't slow down. Warnings are your Ten Commandments; injuries are your sins that you violated with warnings from God' commandments. Death may lead to your reward being lifted unto heaven. Also death may lead to your downfall in Satan's pit in hell. The asterisk symbol (*) is for direction only.

Keep All Eyes on Jesus

Song (A)

While thinking back to the crucifixion of Jesus
I couldn't help but to see
That some people were looking down at their feet
Like in shame or very doubtful to the crucifying of Christ.
Don't pretend to love Jesus and love Satan late at night.
Don't pretend to care about me and talk about me behind
    my back.
To me, you are just wasting time.
(Ch) Keep all eyes on Jesus!
If you can talk about Jesus, then I know you can talk about me.
Listen, if you care, then look me in the eye.
Just like you would if seeing the crucifying of Christ.
If you love me and you care
Be man or woman enough to tell me so.
Most importantly
(Ch) Keep your eyes on Jesus!
By focusing on Jesus, then heaven might be one night away.
(Ch) Keep your eyes on our Lord!
If you love Jesus, then I know that you love me.
Most importantly
You care about me.
(Ch) Keep your eyes on Jesus!

Listen
For the ones that spit/spat on Jesus
For the ones that mocked him
For the ones that crucified our Lord.
One day, they will see our Lord again as prophesied.
(Ch) Keep all eyes on Jesus!
By looking down, then your eyes are focused on hell.
If you love Jesus, then be man or woman enough to tell him so.
Jesus, I love you so much.
*Look up!
And I am not ashamed to tell you so.
Blessings be to all
While all eyes are upon
Your holy name.

Comment

The asterisk is for direction only.

Song (B)

While imagining my Lord and Savior on the cross.
It is very hard to keep the tears from running down my face.
At the same time, trying not to blink my eyes, as if, not to miss
    the spitting, mocking, and facing the sentencing handed to
    our Lord.
This is why we must
(Ch) Keep all eyes on Jesus!
As I watched my Lord, I pray for the ones that don't know
For the reasoning to why you are on the cross.
If it is not too late
I hope that they
(Ch) Keep all eyes on Jesus!
My eyes are upon you, Jesus
My tears just keep on coming
The more I wipe, the more tears seem to come.
I am afraid to blink

Because I may miss the hour and the minute
That you left us.
But I know that is not so
Because our Bible says, "That you would never leave us
Or forsake us."
This is why I must
(Ch) Keep all eyes on your holy name!
As prophesied, our Lord will come again like a thief in the night.
Therefore, my eyes would have blinked many times.
But my focus remains on Jesus's holy name.
Right now, is everyone focused?
(Ch) We are focused!
Don't tell me, tell Jesus.
(Ch) Jesus, we are focused on your holy name.
Tell him like you mean it.
(Ch) Jesus, my Lord and Savior
(Ch) We are focused on your holy name.
Yes, Lord, we all are focused, right now
Right now, Jesus!

Crazy about Jesus

Psalm 54:1–2 says, "Save me, O God, by your name; vindicate
me by your might.
Hear my prayer, O God; listen to the words of my mouth."
From my mouth, my prayers start like this
But there are reasons for my prayers if I am to be crazy for
someone
I'd rather be crazy for Jesus.
(Ch) Why, Jesus?
So you didn't know that no one
Was worthy on earth to be sacrificed for our sins
But then came our Lord and Savior named Jesus.
That's why I'd rather, rather be crazy, crazy for Jesus.
(Ch) What about salvation?
No one was worthy to die for our salvation
But my Lord and Savior named Jesus.
That's why I'd rather, rather be crazy, crazy for Jesus.
(Ch) What about death?
My Jesus has already conquered death
Yes, he did; it was for us to live through eternity.
(Ch) What about the blind?
My Jesus did give sight to the sightless.
(Ch) What about the deaf-mute?

My Jesus did give voice to the voiceless.
That's why I'd rather be crazy, crazy for Jesus.
My Jesus is worthy to be praised and worshipped
Do you all hear what I'm saying?
(Ch) What about the storms?
There is no storm greater than he that my Jesus
Can't take me, can't take me through.
(Ch) What you say!
My Lord can take me through any storm.
This is why I'd rather be crazy for Jesus.
(Ch) Sounds like joy being defined, who would you rather be
    crazy for?
Not the devil, I hope…not!
I can see that some of you are still undecided
Don't you, don't you wait too long
Life is too short; do you hear what I'm saying?
(Ch) Yes, yes, I will start my prayer tonight.
Right now is a good time
Don't wait until the night
It may be too late, my brethren.
If I were you, I would bless his name, right now I did say.
(Ch) Save me, O God, by your name; vindicate me by your
    might
(Ch) Hear my prayer, O God; listen to the words of my mouth.
Save me, save me from all my enemies.
(Ch) Yes, I'd rather be crazy for Jesus

(Repeat)

(Ch) Sorry that it took as long as it did, yes, my Lord!
O God, I thank you for Jesus and for his undying love for me
Let every heart that feels the same way say Amen!

Comments

Psalm 54 is a seven-verse prayer, when the Ziphites had gone to Saul and said, "Is not David hiding among us?" This is the Old Testament, and Jesus came later in order to get to the Father. I only gave two verses of this prayer for deliverance from enemies who wanted to have David killed. Instead of David, I was thinking of myself; while on earth, Jesus gave sight to the sightless, sound to the soundless, conquered death by restoring life to three people and his resurrection. He predicted his death numerous times, and he did not try to get away to save himself; by today's society, that would make him crazy. Today, when you say "bad" but you mean "good" in reference to character, why would I not want to be crazy for my Lord since he was crazy for me? One word does sum up my crazy feelings for the Lord, and that is joy. An example looks like this: undying love for (crazy) + (plus) Jesus = (equal) joy. If you all are still lost, just read about Paul. He didn't care about anything but the kingdom of heaven. Paul was a righteous man. *Paul* can also be found in the *Holman QuickSource Bible Dictionary*.

Jesus, the Only Way to the Father

Song

> **If everyone could close their eyes for a few minutes.
> Just imagine that you are there watching Jesus being crucified
>   on the cross.
> While on the cross, Jesus never mumbled a word.
> So now if I may, I will give voice to his holy name.
> (Ch) Yes, Lord! Yes, Lord! Yes, Jesus, speak to me!
> * "I am the way and the truth and the life.
> No one comes to the Father except through me.
> If you know me, then you will know my Father."
> (Ch) Yes, Lord! Yes, Lord! I know the name of Jesus!
> "I am your Lord! So why some of you all don't want me?"
> (Ch) We cannot rightly answer you, my Lord Jesus.
> "By believing that I am dying for you and I will rise again.
> You will have everlasting life chosen by me."
> (Ch) Yes, Lord! Yes, Lord! Everlasting life!
> ** "Give Jesus praise, everybody!
> Glory to God, we come to praise the Son of God."
> (Ch) Yes, Lord! We praise you, and we love you, Jesus.
> Brethren, I must ask these questions.
> Who did Jesus die for?
> (Ch) He died for you and for me.
> Do you want everlasting life?

JUST BECAUSE (NEW EDITION)

For only the righteous will inherit Mother Earth.
(Ch) Yes, yes! Yes, I want everlasting life, Jesus!
That is what I truly, truly most desire!
Please, everyone, say, "Yes, Lord, I want Jesus!"
He can't hear you if you truly don't believe in him.
For Jesus is listening, he is everlasting life.
(Ch) Yes, Lord! I believe in you, Jesus.
You are the only way to our heavenly Father!
Yes, Lord! Yes, Lord! Yes, Lord!
I believe that you are sent from heaven.
(Ch) Yes, my Lord! My precious Jesus!
I believe Jesus rose up…from the grave…to save me.
Yes, Father (God), I believe in your Son, called Jesus.
Brethren, open up your eyes now.
If tears don't run down them, then you need to close them again.
Once your eyes reopen again, it was because … of Jesus.
On his holy name!
Brethren
The way to the Father may be just a few minutes away.
So work hard, my brethren, and earn your way for heaven's sake.

Comments

No one on earth was worthy enough to pay for our sins and salvation. The cost was just too high, so God sent Jesus as a sacrificial Lamb for payment in full. This is why Jesus is precious, very rare indeed. John 14:6–7 says that "Jesus is the way and the truth and the life. No one comes to the Father except through *him*." "If you really know me, you will know my Father as well." Only a small part of this song is giving voice as Jesus; the other part is from myself. While on earth, many of us spend a great time making earth our home. But there is another home that is more than equally important. That is heaven, my brethren! This song reflects my beliefs and desire for heaven; if you don't prepare, then hell awaits you. Heaven is not given; you must earn your way. Asterisk (*) shown is Jesus speaking.

Asterisks (**) shown is myself speaking.

How are you earning your way?

Are You Serving Two Masters?

First testimonial

In my youth, I went to clubs and bars.

On Sunday morning, I was ready for church.

Now, I only go to church and have Bible study alone; it was hard serving two masters. My experiences only gave me insight and helped me to make a choice for the greater good; when you are ready, God can still use you even if it is for a short time. Once you have chosen to leave those foolish things behind, you are on God's payroll full-time. Always remember, God is never in clubs or bars.

Satan is king there.

On Sunday morning, as you prepare to go to Sunday school or church, remember this: Satan's influence is still over you.

In church, the Spirit must be asked to enter.

If the Spirit never enters church, then the building is not a church at all.

It was the services that Jesus was referring to and not the building. "Upon this rock, I build my church" was Jesus's only church as building and services. Jesus was man and Lord. After his death (resurrection), the Son of Man was no more, but the Son of God remained. Churches these days that don't offer spiritual guidance are not the churches that Jesus envisioned. For example, weddings, funerals, child christenings, and baptisms are just a few services. If your pastors pray to rebuke the devil, he/she can't do it alone.

If two or more good hearts pray for the Spirit, God will enter. Only to the righteous can he be felt. Services are about to begin; we, as God's children, learn at different times where our help does come from.

Upon entering any place of worship, although Satan is not welcome, he can come in and be seated next to you.

Your faith alone will keep Satan at bay.

If faith be your shield, never drop your guard; Satan is less than an ear away.

Are you serving two masters?

Second testimonial

It is easy to be misled and hear phrases taken out of context. For instance, "An eye for an eye, a tooth for a tooth" doesn't mean to return evil for evil.

Please read Matthew 5:38–42 and Luke 6:27–31 for your own understanding. If you return evil for evil, your master is Lucifer (i.e., Satan/devil).

If you return good for evil, your master in heaven will bless and reward you.

This is God!

The question is "which master are you serving?"

Amen!

Comments

I would like to remind any readers that my interpretation is how I understand and accept Christ as my Savior. My songs are based on my understanding. The end result to my understanding is that I do believe in Christ Jesus and he will come again. I do not strive to be perfect, but I do strive to be in God's kingdom.

The songs, poems, and testimonials written are just a few of many for your enjoyment. *Just Because* is just a sample of songs, poems, etc. May God bless you and keep you, my brethren!

The End